W9-BDC-689

Focus On

Children

· ·

A Handbook for Teachers

by Dick Gruber

Gospel Publishing House
Springfield, Missouri
02–0405

Some Scripture quotations are taken from the HOLY BIBLE: NEW
INTERNATIONAL VERSION. © 1973, 1978, 1984 by the International Bible
Society. Used by permission of Zondervan Bible Publishers.

© 1993 by Gospel Publishing House, Springfield, Missouri 65802–1894. All
rights reserved. No part of this book may be reproduced, stored in a retrieval
system, or transmitted in any form or by any means—electronic, mechanical,
photocopy, recording, or otherwise—without prior written permission of the
copyright owner, except brief quotations used in connection with reviews in
magazines or newspapers.

Library of Congress Catalog Card Number 93–078160
International Standard Book Number 0–88243–405–5
Printed in the United States of America

Contents

Foreword

We must focus on children because the Lord commands it when He said, "Suffer little children to come unto me, and forbid them not" (Matthew 19:13). Kids belong in the Kingdom and He prays that we would feed His lambs. They are trusting, believing, and receptive.

We cannot forget them when we think of evangelism and discipleship. These are the ones we must introduce to Jesus and these are also the first to say, "Yes," to God. If the church is to survive the days ahead we cannot forsake the vital task of discipling our young people who will inherit the church of tomorrow.

In an age when kids too often are neglected, abandoned, and abused; the church needs to assure them that there is a mighty God upon whom they can depend. We need to meet their need for love, security and, above all, spiritual values. Christians should know how to present Christ's salvation and lordship.

If you are concerned for the future of our faith you have to be concerned for the children. They need you to show them to Jesus. Let this book help you focus on these little ones.

BOB HAHN
CHILDREN'S PASTOR
FIRST ASSEMBLY OF GOD
JOLIET, ILLINOIS

Why Teach Children?

"Train a child in the way he should go, and when he is old he will not turn from it" (Proverbs 22:6). "Jesus said, 'let the little children come to me, and do not hinder them, for the kingdom of heaven belongs to such as these'" (Matthew 19:14).

These directives of Scripture reveal the importance of reaching, teaching, winning, and discipling children. Although Scripture designates the home as primary in this spiritual training, the role of Sunday school has become increasingly important.

In many cases the home has, through indifference or outright anti-Christian sentiment, failed to provide proper training. The Sunday school has become the "spiritual home" to many children in our country today.

In the Sunday school and related ministries, a child can find friends, acceptance, and a relationship with Jesus Christ.

An elderly teacher in Rochester, New York walked up to me after a workshop and said, "Remember son, you don't teach lessons, you teach individuals." These individuals which God has given you differ in physical appearance, mental ability, socialization skills, and spiritual understanding.

In this era of broken and blended families, committed and noncommitted Christians, you will have students that eagerly attend your class weekly. There will be others, because of family circumstances, that fall into sporadic attendance patterns.

Every individual that steps into the Sunday school classroom craves individual attention and unconditional acceptance.

Some churches have mistakenly dropped Sunday school in favor of "Super Church." Others have weighed the expense of Sunday school for children against other church expenditures and wondered if the cost was justifiable. Let me assure you, children need Sunday school!

Sunday school provides boys and girls with the essential ingredients for proper Christian living. Some of these essentials include the following: Small group age-level fellowship, regular systematic study of biblical doctrine, ministry training, and the building of good habits in church attendance.

Boys and girls need small-group age-level fellowship. A child, like an adult, needs interaction with those at a similar level of development. Peer approval and friendship are important aspects in a child's healthy social development. In the small group age-level class, age appropriate music, methods, and activities bring life to the gospel message.

Regular systematic study of Bible doctrine cannot be emphasized enough. Children must receive systematic doctrinal training throughout the elementary years. Sunday school provides this doctrinal training. Children's church, and club programs reinforce the doctrinal foundation that Sunday school constructs. Radiant Life curriculum establishes a systematic full gospel pattern of doctrinal study for our children's Sunday school classes.

Ministry training is an ongoing process. This begins in the early childhood class as a boy or a girl helps the teacher hand out snacks, or prays for his friend who has an *owie*. In the elementary level, children need to be actively involved in each class session. Children are part of the body of Christ, the Church. They can minister to one another. The elementary child can tell a Bible story, lead a song, or lead in prayer. Sunday school is the ideal place for ongoing ministry training.

"What then shall we say, brothers? When you come together, everyone has a hymn, or a word of instruction, a revelation, a tongue, or an interpretation. All of these must be done for the strengthening of the church" (1 Corinthians 14:26).

This book is not an all-inclusive training manual. Volumes could be written on each subject introduced herein. Treat this as an introduction to your ministry with children.

You will learn how to better reach, teach, win, disciple, and send the boys and girls of your class. Philosophy and methodology will be woven together giving you basic tools; tools sharpened for immediate use in the Sunday school of your church.

It is the prayer of this writer that you devour this first course in that meal called training. Enjoy it, relish it, and then move on to the rest of the menu. Training books, magazines, (e.g., *Sunday School Counselor*), and events are available to you on a local and national level. Continue learning all you can so that the children you serve may enjoy quality and exciting instruction in the Word of God.

"Whoever gives heed to instruction prospers, and blessed is he who trusts in the Lord" (Proverbs 16:20). "Listen to advice and accept instruction, and in the end you will be wise" (Proverbs 19:20).

Why Sunday School?

"During the Wesleyan revival of the 18th century in England, a printer from Gloucester was burdened to do something to help the poor children of his city. His name was Robert Raikes. He began to bring the children to his home on Sundays. There, he taught them reading skills, using the Bible as his textbook."[1]

From those humble beginnings, a man who simply wanted to make a difference in the lives of children founded the modern Sunday school movement. Since those first Sundays in England, Sunday school has spread worldwide, preparing the saints for works of ministry. Sunday school may be a relatively young movement, but training in God's Word is as old as Scripture itself.

Deuteronomy 4:9 says, "Only be careful, and watch yourselves closely so that you do not forget the things your eyes have seen or let them slip from your heart as long as you live. Teach them to your children and to their children after them."

In Deuteronomy 6:6,7 we are encouraged, "These commandments that I give you today are to be upon your hearts. Impress them on your children. Talk about them when you sit at home and when you walk along the road, when you lie down and when you get up."

"Train a child in the way he should go, and when he is old he will not turn from it" (Proverbs 22:6). The Bible training of a child was once centered in his home. Today, with so many broken and blended families, little or no time is spent in the home studying God's Word. Even the child raised in a "Christian" home may see little of the Bible between Sundays.

The Sunday school has become the primary place of evangelism and teaching in our culture today.

One Sunday my daughter Rachel, who was then 6 years old, shared with me her Sunday school experience. "Dad", she exclaimed, "Jesus said that if someone wants you to carry his backpack a mile you should carry it two miles."

Proud of the grasp my daughter had on the lesson of the day I questioned, "What do you think this means for your life, Rachel?"

She pondered the message for a moment and said, "I guess Christians are good at carrying backpacks."

What is the purpose of Sunday school for children? Is it a place of doctrinal training or is it babysitting? Are children simply encouraged to repeat rote recitations or are lessons related to everyday living?

As already mentioned, Sunday school provides children with small group age-level fellowship, regular systematic study of biblical doctrine, ministry training, and the building of good habits in church attendance.

Sunday school also provides children with a place where they can "learn how to interact with love and trust, to respect people, and to appreciate a variety of personalities, achievements, and contributions."[2]

A quality Sunday school for the children will establish lifelong patterns of faith and experience. A quality Sunday school for the children will draw them to your church again and again. The child who burns with Sunday school enthusiasm, many times drags mom or dad to church each week until the Sunday school flame ignites excitement in his parents' heart.

Seven basic Sunday school objectives are listed by *Radiant Life Curriculum*.[3]

1. Salvation
2. Biblical Knowledge

3. Spirit-Filled Life
4. Christian Growth
5. Personal Commitment
6. Christian Service
7. Christian Living

Each of these objectives applies to the elementary Sunday school experience.

SALVATION

Help each student to accept Christ. "He came to that which was his own, but his own did not receive him. Yet to all who received him, to those who believed in his name, he gave the right to become children of God" (John 1:11,12). Jesus said, "Let the little children come to me, and do not hinder them, for the kingdom of heaven belongs to such as these" (Matthew 19:14). "Whoever believes and is baptized will be saved, but whoever does not believe will be condemned" (Mark 16:16). "And everyone who calls on the name of the Lord will be saved" (Acts 2:21).

The whoever and the everyone of Scripture is not exclusively written to adults. God's desire is that all men would seek him.

Romans 10:9 states, "That if you confess with your mouth, "Jesus is Lord," and believe in your heart that God raised him from the dead, you will be saved."

I don't understand how much a first grader may understand, but I do know that you can present Christ to him. The elementary Sunday school must be a place of evangelism. Children must be given the opportunity to believe on the Lord Jesus.

Teaching for Decision, by Richard Dresselhaus contains a wonderful chapter explaining the concept of the age of accountability.

He writes, "Paul points to the individuality of man's responsibility to God and suggests, at least by influence, that at some point every man is compelled to consider the claims of God upon his life. The time of accountability is the moment of grace when one is brought to a decision for or against Christ by the Spirit."[4]

Pastor Dresselhaus provides biblical and cultural background to the idea of the age of accountability, then includes the following statements in his treatise: "Obviously it is impossible to determine a uniform age when all children reach this point of awareness. Regardless of the child's age, the necessary element for accepting Christ is understanding both his need for salvation and Christ's ability to save him."[5]

When should a child be approached about making a personal commitment to Christ? In answering this question, Pastor Dresselhaus writes, "Periodically, as the Spirit directs, a child should be approached about a personal relationship with Christ. If the time is right, the Holy Spirit will continue to direct, and the child's response will indicate a readiness to receive Christ. However, a child should never be pushed or coerced into a spiritual experience."[6]

BIBLICAL KNOWLEDGE

Help each student hear, understand, believe, and obey the Bible. The Bible is the official textbook for Sunday schools. But the Bible must be more than a book we study on Sunday mornings. The Bible must come to life for boys and girls. They must receive its message in a way that is understandable to them and be given the opportunity to respond.

In his book, *The Sunday School Spirit*, Stephen Rexroat gives three words basic to this concept: *know, feel*, and *do*. "The word *know* is a cognitive goal and deals with what the student must know and the information he must possess to make the proper decision. *Feel* is the word we use to identify the affective goal or the way the student must feel to respond properly. *Do* is the word we use to define the desired behavior or acceptable response."[7]

If a child is to act upon the directives of God's Word, he must first have a knowledge of those directives and feel a need to act. Sunday school must provide biblical knowledge, and the motivation to act upon that knowledge, in ways that are understandable to boys and girls whatever their age-level.

SPIRIT-FILLED LIFE

Help each student receive the baptism in the Holy Spirit and maintain a daily walk with the Spirit. There are some adults who are of the opinion that children are too young to understand the depth of this experience we call the baptism in the Holy Spirit. I ask you, "Can you understand the full implications of this powerful immersion?" Your lack of understanding all of the theological implications did not hinder you from seeking to receive all that God has for you.

On the day of Pentecost, Peter said, "The promise is for you and your children and for all who are far off—for all whom the Lord our God will call" (Acts 2:39). He was referring to the promise of the Holy Spirit! Yes, children can be filled with the Spirit! "For everyone who asks receives; he who seeks finds; and to him who knocks, the door will be opened. Which of you fathers, if your son asks for a fish, will give him a snake instead? Or if he asks for an egg, will give him a scorpion? If you then, though you are evil, know how to give good gifts to your children, how much more will your Father in heaven give the Holy Spirit to those who ask him!" (Luke 11:10–13).

A Sunday school teacher in South Dakota came to a Radiant Life Middler lesson on the baptism in the Holy Spirit. She taught and prayed for the children in her third-grade class. Every child was filled with the Spirit! God is no respecter of persons. He wants to move in the fullness of the Spirit in your elementary class.

CHRISTIAN GROWTH

Help each student grow into Christian maturity. Paul writes, "We loved you so much that we were delighted to share with you not only the gospel of God but our lives as well, because you had become so dear to us" (1 Thessalonians 2:8).

Paul was describing the kind of Sunday school teacher that spurs children on to continued growth in Christ. You can be that kind of Sunday school teacher! I believe that every student will grow a little more like Jesus in each class they attend. Begin praying and believing for Christian growth in the lives of your students.

PERSONAL COMMITMENT

Help each student totally commit his life to the will of God. God's will is that all should not perish but have everlasting life. Training children in the way they should go is an ongoing process. A child who totally commits himself to Christ today will continue to reach higher steps of spiritual, mental, and emotional cognizance. As a child reaches deeper levels of understanding, he will undoubtedly feel the need to recommit his life to Christ.

CHRISTIAN SERVICE

Help each student find and fulfill his place of service as a member of the body of Christ. If we believe that a child can be saved, then it follows that the same child has a place of service in the family of God. Children have ministry gifts. The wise teacher will seek to discover each child's gifts or abilities and capitalize on these in lesson preparation and presentation.

CHRISTIAN LIVING

Help each student apply Christian principles to every relationship and duty of life. A child is never too young to begin serving God in everyday living. The concrete thinking firstgrader may not comprehend the omnipresence of Jesus, but he can, for God's glory, clean his room or help his mother do dishes. Paul wrote to the Colossians, "And whatever you do, whether in word or deed, do it all in the name of the Lord Jesus, giving thanks to God the Father through him" (Colossians 3:17). Later in the chapter he writes, "Whatever you do, work at it with all your heart, as working for the Lord, not for men, since you know that you will receive an inheritance from the Lord as a reward. It is the Lord Christ you are serving" (Colossians 3:23–24).

Sunday school can be a place of continued encouragement for the child who wants to serve Jesus. Your life of service will have a profound effect on the children you serve. Sunday school is the flour tortilla which holds the ingredients of doctrinal training and experience. Sunday school is the hub of that wheel which is called church ministries. Sunday school constitutes the most important church based hour in a child's weekly spiritual growth.

Why Sunday school? I say why not! Sunday school is still the main thrust of systematic doctrinal training for the children of our churches. "Careful planning, cooperative effort, efficient leadership, and total dedication are the ingredients of aggressive, successful, Sunday schools." In *First Steps For Teachers*, Bill Martin says, "Teacher, you can be the most exciting person, the Bible can be the most exciting book, and Sunday school can be the most exciting hour in a child's week."[8]

Me, A Teacher?

"Then he went down to Capernaum, a town in Galilee, and on the Sabbath began to teach the people" (Luke 4:31).

J esus was a Teacher! What an honor for you and me to wear the same title. God has called you into a most important ministry. "It was he who gave some to be apostles, some to be prophets, some to be evangelists, and some to be pastors and teachers, to prepare God's people for works of service, so that the body of Christ may be built up" (Ephesians 4:11,12).

I once had a teacher come up to me and ask, "If God called me, why doesn't He answer the phone?" God has called you to this ministry of teaching. He promises to never leave you or forsake you. He said, " teaching them to obey everything I have commanded you. And surely I am with you always, to the very end of the age" (Matthew 28:20). As one teacher put it, "God's promise to us is lo I am with you always, even till the end of your class."

Every ministry in the church carries with it certain responsibilities. An usher may be required to dress or to speak in a certain manner. A nursery attendant may be expected to enroll in a childcare course at a local community college. Each ministry carries with it a responsibility to the church body, to the church leadership, and most importantly to Christ. Let us look at the *y* and responsibility of the elementary Sunday school

THE MINISTRY

Jesus said, "Feed my lambs" (John 21:15). "Be shepherds of God's flock that is under your care, serving as overseers—not because you must, but because you are willing, as God wants you to be; not greedy for money, but eager to serve; not lording it over those entrusted to you, but being examples to the flock" (1 Peter 5:2,3).

You are a minister of the Gospel. You are a shepherd of His little lambs. It is no accident that you are the chosen one for your Sunday school class. God loves the children of your class so much that He gave them you! Your abilities, your creativity, your personality are matched to that of the children you serve.

A TEACHER

A teacher!
A loving leader of learners, a servant, a friend,
Full of joy, full of love,
Patient, kind, good, godly,
FAITHFUL!
A gentle example
Self-controlled
A person above reproach
In life, in action, in speech
Defender of truth
Dependent on God
Daring to be doing!
Guider of godly growth
A helper

Excited about the good news!
A tour guide to heavenly places
Creative memory maker
Artist of attitudes
Molding minds, helping hurts, hearts
Directing darlings dutifully
Helping, holding, hearing, hoping
Praying, preparing, presenting
God-ordained, God-directed, God-inspected
A teacher

There are 168 hours in a week. Get out a tape measure. Assign 1 inch for every hour. You now have 168 inches or 14 feet. The hour of Sunday school is only 1 inch on that vast length of tape. The average American child views more than 3.5 hours of television each day. (N.C.T.V., Newsletter, 1987)[9] If we use the conservative figure of 3.5 that makes 24.5 hours of television each week. Balance that against the 1 hour spent in your Sunday school class during the same time frame.

If a child attends Sunday school every week during his elementary years he would have been in class 13 accumulated days. During that same time, this child has watched 319.25 days of television.

You have a ministry to the children that must reach beyond the single hour on Sunday morning. The children need to know that you are available to them any time and any day of the week.

Since 1980 I have given my phone number to the children in my class. In all of this time, I have only had two prank phone calls from the kids. On numerous occasions, children have called with prayer requests, testimonies, or just to talk.

One 12-year-old girl from a broken home used to call me at midnight or even 1 A.M. Her mother would be out on a date leaving her to babysit three younger sisters. When her 4- year-old sister had trouble sleeping, the call would come. I told bedtime stories to the 4-year-old, prayed with her, and sent her to bed. I kept the line open and talked with the 12-year-old until her sister was asleep.

Chances are a child who is in need will not have or express that need between 9:30 A.M. and noon on Sunday. Your availability during the week will increase your effectiveness on Sunday morning. You expect your pastor to be available for ministry at all times. The children of your class expect no less from you.

The minister is a person of the Word and of prayer. The importance of your consistency in these vital practices cannot be stressed strongly enough. Your life is an example to the boys and girls whom you serve.

Bob Hahn, Christian educator from Joliet, Illinois, has come up with this practical list for the elementary teacher.[10] Check your life, ministry, and attitudes against this. How do you measure up as a minister to elementary children?

CHILDREN'S STAFF

(A General Ministry Description)

I. Spiritual Qualifications

a. Born Again (John 3:3)
b. Spirit filled or seeking (Acts 1:5,8)
c. Baptized in water (Mark 16:16)
d. Private devotional life (1 Thessalonians 5:17)
e. Consistent Christian life (Colossians 3:5,17)
f. Practice proper principles of giving (Malachi 3:8–12)

II. Church Loyalty

a. Regularly attend church services
b. Submit to churches policies and leaders
c. Be courteous to your coworkers
d. Avoid teaching anything that conflicts with your churches set of beliefs.

III. Attitude

a. See your task as a calling more than a job
b. Your task belongs to God

  c. Your service is for the glory of God
  d. You are part of Christ's body, not an island or separate from the rest of the Body
  e. Never allow a human-level conflict to interfere with your spiritual calling

IV. Christian Life

  a. Live a life consistent with Scripture (2 Timothy 3:16)
  b. Model yourself after Christ to glorify God and to help others to be saved (1 Corinthians 10:31, 11:1)
  c. Purify yourself from everything that contaminates your body or your spirit (2 Corinthians 7:1; i.e., tobacco, drugs, pornography, etc.)
  d. Avoid behavior which would offend another Christian (1 Corinthians 8:9–13)
  e. Avoid the appearance of evil (1 Thessalonians 5:22)

Some churches have added their own section with specifics relevant to their setting. Feel free to adapt this in the context of your church and ministry.

THE RESPONSIBILITY

One Sunday a sixth-grade Sunday school teacher named Dale approached me after the church hour. "I'm sorry, Pastor," he said. "I didn't mean to keep the sixth-grade class all through the church hour. It will never happen again."

"Dale," I questioned. "Why did you keep the class the entire Sunday morning?"

He stuttered apologetically, "This boy invited two friends to our class. At the end of class time, the two visitors gave their lives to Jesus as we prayed. These boys started asking questions and before I knew it, church time was over."

"Dale!" I exclaimed. "Never apologize for a move of God in the lives of children!" A teacher has the responsibility to teach children. When a teachable moment arrives, you cannot ignore or dismiss it. You must act on it and thank God for an opportu-

ılfill your calling.

ːole is one of servanthood and spiritual leadership.
his, you have responsibilities and expectations that
originate from the children, the parents, and the church leadership. Many of these may not be written. Pray for wisdom in regard to these responsibilities. "If any of you lacks wisdom he should ask God, who gives generously to all without finding fault, and it will be given to him" (James 1:5).

Take a look at the responsibilities of the Sunday school teacher. Begin with responsibilities in the classroom. Move to the church, to the home, and finally to the community.

In the Class

The first and most important responsibility is to be there! How can you teach if you are not in the classroom? Many teachers wonder why they have discipline problems. The child who enters an empty Sunday school room will begin class without the teacher. When the teacher finally arrives, this child and others will be involved in presession activities that bare little resemblance to Christian living. Be there, teacher!

If you have arrived and the children are already in the classroom, then you are late. Be there to listen, to talk, and to prepare the environment and the early arrivals for your lesson.

Children expect you to be well prepared, polite, and excited. You have a responsibility to provide a safe enjoyable environment for the children. Look at your classroom. Are there old papers cluttering every countertop? Is some of the furniture dangerous? Does the carpet have a rip down the middle that will trip a child? Do all you can to insure a safe, enjoyable class time.

Involve children in ministry in your classroom. Trusting a child with minor tasks, often builds his self-esteem. Children learn much more and retain what they have learned much longer when they are actively involved in the Sunday school experience.

Out of Class

It is important for every teacher to attend services or classes at times other than their appointed ministry. Whenever possible, attend services at your church. This will be of benefit to the child who observes and interacts with you and will be refreshing to your spirit.

When you see a child from class in the halls of the church, both the parents and the child expect your fellowship. I make it a practice to shake a child's hand and speak to him before addressing the parents. Children will stay and listen if you show them proper consideration and care.

Once again, I stress, "Be There!" Your faithful model will inspire children and their parents.

One Sunday evening I observed children waiting by the door of our church. When questioned, I discovered that these little ones were waiting for their Sunday school teacher. They knew she would soon arrive and they wanted to share a testimony. The child will watch you give tithes and offerings. He will listen to your talk with other adults, your worship, and your prayers. He will pray with and for you at the altars.

The Home and the Community

The Sunday school teacher can have an impact on the lifestyles of his students and their families. Visiting students in the home, at athletic events, and at the local ice cream parlor lays a foundation for lasting results.

The teacher should always travel with another teacher or helper when visiting students. Jesus sent his followers out by twos. "Calling the Twelve to him, he sent them out two by two and gave them authority over evil spirits" (Mark 6:7). "After this the Lord appointed seventy-two others and sent them two by two ahead of him to every town and place where he was about to go" (Luke 10:1).

I was walking through a local department store, and just as I passed the toy section a young boy ran up to me smiling and screaming, "Mom, dad! This is the guy who teaches children's church." This boy was one of our bus children, so I spent a little time talking to his parents. After several visits to their home, this couple began attending church with their son.

A teacher is responsible to live the Christian life everywhere he goes. What a tragedy for a child to witness his Sunday school teacher angrily berate a clerk at the local grocery store. The children in your class may see you at the library, the video store, or a baseball game. These children watch and learn what you are living. "But if anyone causes one of these little ones who believe in me to sin, it would be better for him to have a large millstone hung around his neck and to be drowned in the depths of the sea" (Matthew 18:6).

Become an active part of the child's life beyond the classroom. This is your responsibility, your calling. By doing this you become a giver of a drink of water.

"And if anyone gives even a cup of cold water to one of these little ones because he is my disciple, I tell you the truth, he will certainly not lose his reward" (Matthew 10:42).

To Fellow Workers and To the Church

Another area of responsibility that cannot be ignored is to your fellow workers and to your church. A Sunday school teacher must be loyal to leadership and to other staff members. If you have a difficulty with a fellow worker or pastor, the biblical thing to do is to take it directly to that worker or pastor.

"If your brother sins against you, go and show him his fault, just between the two of you. If he listens to you, you have won your brother over" (Matthew 18:15). Never allow a human-level conflict to undermine your ministry. Your loyalty to your fellow laborers and to your church will transfer to the children you serve.

I have always felt the responsibility to pray for my fellow workers and for my church and its leadership. Pray for the other ministries of the church also. Once again, you are modeling unity of purpose to the children in your class.

Clean up your own mess! How many times have you entered a classroom and become enraged at the teacher who left your room a disaster area? Cleaning up at the end of snack or activity time, teaches the children a love and respect for God's house and for those who will use the classroom next.

Your ministry and your responsibilities as outlined in this

chapter and in Scripture are of awesome proportion. A look at the eternal significance of your task could be overwhelming.

You look at yourself in a mirror and say, "How could I be the kind of servant described here? How can I become what God desires for my elementary students?" With God all things are possible (Matthew 19:26). Colossians 1:29 says, "To this end I labor, struggling with all his energy, which so powerfully works in me." In *The Living Bible* it states, "This is my work, and I can do it only because Christ's mighty energy is at work within me."

The Lord understands your abilities and your weaknesses. He will always be there to strengthen you and to grant you wisdom. His mighty energy will be at work in you each time you enter the classroom. As you faithfully prepare your lessons, Jesus will provide you with a supernatural anointing for ministry.

Teacher, you must arrive at a place of total dependence on God. You must strive to sharpen your abilities, your tools for ministry, and then let God finish the work.

Jesus, the master teacher is by your side. As you strive to become an example of His love to the children of your class, the Holy Spirit will give you power and wisdom. His desire for your success is demonstrated by his availability to meet your needs. If God called you, he will be there when you call him!

I visited a Sunday school class in a church in Virginia one Sunday and marveled at the efficiency of the teaching team. That's right, I said, "teaching team." As a matter of fact, a team of teachers served in every classroom I entered that Sunday morning.

There are many good reasons to team up with one or more believers in your teaching. Regardless of class size, a team can make the Sunday school experience more enjoyable for both teachers and students. Let's look at some reasons for the team teaching concept in your Sunday school.

- ■ Jesus' example- In Luke chapter 10, we find Jesus sending out disciples in groups of two. There is something wonderful about having a fellow laborer in the harvest field.

■ Common Sense—There is safety in numbers. In today's society, it makes good sense for the teacher to have an assistant. It is too easy for the world to bring an accusation against the church or the teacher. One family crying, "Child abuse," can ruin your life and your ministry. Having an assistant in the room with you reduces the risk of accusation. Flee the very appearance of evil.

■ Discipline—Classroom discipline is easier with an assistant. One instructs, while the other ministers discipline to a needy child. Two adults can better control an elementary classroom. If a child has an especially hard day, your assistant can minister to him while you continue with the lesson.

■ Relating to the individual—There is a better chance of two different personalities being able to relate to individual needs. At times a child may relate to the assistant more than to the lead teacher. Different faces and personalities create more interest for the students.

■ Accountability—The teacher may spend more time in preparation if there is another adult in the room. Every teacher should prepare properly out of love for God and the children, but another adult seems to motivate many to a higher standard of excellence.

■ Follow-up—This is always a concern to the conscientious teacher. With a team, one can teach while others are recording attendance and/or writing cards or letters to absentees.

■ Prayer—There is strength in the prayers of two or more believers. One can silently pray for the one who is teaching. The team members can call one another during the week and offer prayer support. What a thrill it is to teach in a class that offers this kind of spiritual support.

- The Unexpected—Sometimes the unexpected happens, even in Sunday school. When emergencies occur, the team can handle the problem while maintaining order. In one class a 3-year-old tripped and scraped his chin and nose on a brick wall. Two members of the teaching team calmed the worried classmates while the third member cared for the injured child.

- Discipleship—A team relationship is ideal for discipling future teachers. The disciple, or assistant, is learning from his leader every time class meets. Being an assistant in a Sunday school class gives practical experience to a teacher in training.

- Response—During response time one teacher can pray with the children who wish to respond. The other teacher works with children who have not responded. Other team members may lead in a song, or pray with and for the students.

Where do churches find team members? Some are recruiting senior saints. These wise grandpas and grandmas are finding a new joy in service to children. Every church has a few seniors who want to feel needed and every child needs spiritual grandparents.

Others are looking to the youth department for quality assistants. Many teens feel a call to ministry. The Sunday school class is a wonderful place to fulfill that call until that young person can move into full-time ministry. A teen should not be left attending children without adult supervision. There must always be an adult present in the Sunday school classroom.

One member of the team should take charge. This lead teacher is responsible for control of the room, assigning parts of the lesson to other teachers, and obtaining materials needed in the class. This person is an experienced teacher. Members should compliment each other. For example, a good storyteller can be teamed up with a song leader who may not have any storytelling skills.

My desire for you is that you would not have to serve alone in the classroom. Teaching on a team will be a rewarding experience for you and the children. Pray to the Lord of the harvest. Then work with your Sunday school superintendent. Together you will discover and recruit team members who will perfectly suit the children you serve.

JESUS, THE MASTER TEACHER

Practics

1. He believed what He taught.
2. He had authority and confidence in His teaching.
3. He knew the Scriptures.
4. He understood His pupils.
5. He understood how to teach.
6. He believed in teaching.
7. He exhibited the fruit of the Spirit.

Pupils

1. He met the students where they were at.
2. He taught for life-change.
3. He accepted people as they were.
4. He always lifted students to a higher ideal.

Purposes

1. He sought to convert His pupils to God.
2. He tried to develop good self esteem in His pupils.
3. He instilled right ideals in the learner.
4. He sought to deepen one's convictions.
5. He trained others to carry on His teachings.

Presentations

1. He used a variety of methodology.
2. He used concrete terms.
3. He used visuals.
4. He involved pupils in the learning process.
5. He taught in a way that was easy to understand.

Compare the information on this chart to your practices as a Sunday school teacher. Your first thought may be, "Jesus could do and be all of that because He was God." Our Lord was also fully man, and in his humanity taught those around him using methodology that any teacher can utilize. In this, He provides an example that is possible for us to imitate.

What Are They Made Of? 4

Wouldn't it be boring if every child was exactly the same? God must have thought so to create such diversity. Children come in a variety of shapes and sizes, and physical and mental abilities. Individuals you serve are growing in body and understanding at different velocities.

In the next chapter we will discuss the importance and practics of building relationships with these individuals. Before we can do this, we must first lay a foundation of general characteristics of each age-level. To effectively minister to a child, you must know some of the characteristics common to his age-level.

This chapter cannot list all attributes of every age-level. What it can include are general characteristics that will assist you in better understanding the children you serve. This understanding will enhance your effectiveness in your lesson planning and in your presentation.

After studying the characteristics of the age-level you teach, you will want to observe your students. You should begin to recognize the different characteristics. Recognizing these will better equip you for Christlike classroom management.

PRIMARIES

They come in different shapes, sizes, and colors. Some are 6-years-old, and some are 7- years-old. They are Primary children.

Most will be in first- or second-grade at the local school.

Some have said, "These are the years of constant motion." Others have labeled these "the questioning years." Primary-aged children constantly move through their environment questioning everything and everybody.

Physical Characteristics

Body development, muscle coordination, stamina, good health, and motor skills are all part of a child's physical characteristics. These characteristics are important to you as a children's worker because they place limitations on both the amount of time and the type of classroom activities you may use. Knowing what the child is able to do physically will eliminate frustration; both yours and the students'.

Three important similarities common to 6- and 7-year-olds are an abundance of energy, restlessness, and tiring easily.

The Primary child is full of energy. He is constantly moving from one activity to the next. The Primary likes to try new things, provided they aren't too difficult. A variety of activities both stationary and mobile will capture his interest and help channel this energy in a positive direction.

Restlessness is caused by muscle development. As muscles are developing, they feel tense and achy when not in use. A child will squirm and wiggle to stretch his muscles. The child does not know why he experiences the need to move, he only knows that he must move in order to feel comfortable.

A wise teacher will shuffle classroom activities so that a quiet segment is followed by movement and stretching followed by calm and so on. Do not attempt to keep Primary children in one position in their seats through the entire Sunday school lesson. To do so is to work against the manufacturer's warranty.

Since children expend much energy in constant movement, it is only natural that they tire easily. Sometimes after strenuous work, children need rest. Through the rest period they rebuild energy levels for continued movement. Do not expect all children to need the same amount of rest at the same time. In light of this, you may wish to plan a mandatory rest/quiet time during each class period.

Here are some general and specific characteristics of 6-and 7-year olds.

Mental Characteristics

Mental characteristics of Primaries are harder to openly observe in the classroom. Only their results can be seen. A Sunday school teacher should not judge one child superior to another on the basis of the mental characteristics they observe. All children should have the same opportunities to learn and to develop in Sunday school.

Primary-aged children are concrete thinkers. Avoid abstract symbolism or illustrations. When a teacher talks about asking Jesus to come into your heart, the 6-or 7-year-old may believe that Jesus is actually entering the blood pumping organ. The concrete mind-set may have difficulty understanding concepts such as omnipresence, or the blood of Jesus cleansing us from all unrighteousness. Do not shy away from theology or questions, but learn to listen to the child and to explain eternal truths in simple understandable "concrete" terminology.

Most Primaries live in a frame of reference that deals with the here and now. They have limited concepts of time, space, and distance. Quite often they will mix up Old and New Testament characters. They are not able to grasp the wide span of time that the Bible covers.

Although Jesus lived almost 2000 years ago, He is their friend today. To a Primary, Jesus didn't live that long ago. The concept of the future is also confusing to children. Two or three days is a long time to most Primaries.

Added to their limited concepts of time and space is a limited concept of distance. They do not understand the distance that separates them from Israel or what a 3-day journey in biblical times meant. Primaries do not understand maps and the distances they represent. A teacher should introduce children to Bible geography, but do not expect the children to understand the details it may represent.

Primaries are curious. They want to know why things happen.

Since their vocabulary is limited, they enjoy feeling or seeing a picture or object rather than just hearing about it. If you do not want children to touch an object, do not bring it to class.

Social Characteristics

A whole new world is beginning to open to the Primary. He is expanding his world of relationships through attending elementary school, extracurricular activities, and Sunday school. He has progressed from a world where he was the center of attention to a world where friends play an important role. The result of this change is that the Primary begins to develop a different outlook on life and friendships.

Primaries want to be accepted. They want to be accepted first by their peers, and secondly by adults. Even at the age of six peer pressure is beginning to control the child. It is important that the Primary child be accepted by the other class members or he may become withdrawn.

Several other problems are associated with this acceptance. Most Primaries do not know how to make or to keep a friend. If you observe children, you will find that some children hit others. It's their way of expressing friendship. Other children become class clowns. Their security comes from making people laugh.

As a Sunday school teacher, you may need to explain to the children how to make friends. Children can be extremely cruel in what they say to one another. Part of your task is to maintain control of the classroom setting. Do not allow a child or a group of children to pick on other class members. In like manner, you must never make fun of or embarrass a child. Sunday school is a place where every child should be lifted up, where every child can succeed.

Primaries are just learning to compete with others for the attention of adults. You will find these children very talkative. They talk a lot because they want to impress you and want you to know who they are. Many of the things they talk about will be exaggerated. Rather than embarrass them in front of their peers, listen carefully and sort out the fact from the fantasy.

Because a lot of fantasy is often connected with what the

Primary says, teachers tend to "half listen" to the conversation. In doing so, some of the child's factual comments are missed. Children sense when an adult is not listening. If you want children to listen to you, then you must extend the same courtesy to them.

Emotional Characteristics

The Primary child faces many problems and fears. He is awakening to a much larger world than he has previously known. He is aware of many adult ideas and expectations, but he is still a child and cannot respond like an adult.

Children today face pressure and temptation unlike any we faced as children. Home life is often unstable. Many have become latch-key children. Over half the children in America are directly impacted by divorce. Children are put in a position of caring for their own needs for sometimes as much as 5 hours a day. As a result, boys and girls are forced to take responsibilities and make decisions that exceed their emotional development.

The right friends, the right clothes, the right notebook, or the right shoes are all putting undo social and economic pressures on children.

Many children have been or are being exploited sexually by adults. Children are being neglected and abused. The Sunday school teacher must be aware of these concerns and ready to assist the child in need.

The attack on childhood has soared to epidemic proportions. This causes fears, phobias, and stress-related illness among young children. Some children are equipped to cope with all of this, most are not! Each year an increasing number of early elementary children turn to drugs, alcohol, and even suicide to solve their problems in this world that will not allow them to be children.

The Sunday school teacher is going to be facing more and more children who have deep-seated fears. One of the greatest things you can instill in the children is the knowledge that Jesus loves them. He understands confusion, hurt, and guilt.

Primaries need assurance from adults that what they are

doing is all right. For example, a Primary may make a big fuss over pasting a picture in the right place on a take home paper. He just needs your encouragement. He needs to know that you are really paying attention to him and his needs. Proverbs 16:21 says, "The wise in heart are called discerning, and pleasant words promote instruction." Your pleasant words will build a child's self-esteem. Your pleasant words in a personal matter will be remembered when you stand before the class.

Primaries have many worries and fears. Some may seem ridiculous to the teacher, but are very real to the child. I take every prayer request, every worry seriously. The Scriptures encourage the believer to "Cast all your anxiety on him because he cares for you" (1 Peter 5:7). There is no stipulation as to the size of the anxiety or the age of the one casting.

When you encounter a child who is fearful, you need to assure him that a) he is of value; b) you care about him; c) God cares about him; and, d) he is loved unconditionally. Spending a few minutes listening to a child can do much to calm his anxieties.

Primaries are very sensitive to criticism. The teacher should avoid criticizing children in front of their peers. A private talk with a child, avoiding harsh criticism, usually produces positive results. Most Primary children want to please the teacher.

The Primary child will occasionally test the authority of the teacher. Sometimes they do this for attention. Other times a child may want to be the boss and get his own way. A teacher who allows a child to disobey has lost control of that child and of the class. A teacher must have control of his class at all times. Firmness (not harshness), as well as reasonable rules, will help children respect your authority.

Remember, the Primary child is changing rapidly in every way. He is growing emotionally, and like a young flower just opening its petals, is sensitive to extremes around him.

Spiritual Characteristics

Measuring the various stages of a child's spiritual development is difficult. So much at this age depends on the influence or training a child has had in the home. This presents a problem to the Sunday school teacher who must deal with boys and girls of the same age-level but with different backgrounds.

One cannot predict with accuracy the spiritual characteristics of Primary children. It is important for the teacher to follow the leading of the Holy Spirit when ministering to the children in his class. The Holy Spirit will guide you in knowing when a child is ready to make a commitment to Jesus. Never shy away from approaching a child concerning spiritual things. Remember, "Jesus said, 'Let the little children come to me, and do not hinder them, for the kingdom of heaven belongs to such as these'" (Matthew 19:14).

A child should never be forced or coerced into making a spiritual decision. There will come a time when you will want to approach each child individually and discuss their spiritual understanding.

Teaching Primaries can be an enjoyable experience. Keep lesson segments short and interesting. Offer a choice of activities so that the Primary child can choose what he likes to do. Avoid long lectures. Involve the children in the learning experience giving them things to do, things to make, and things to sense. Be aware of the physical, mental, social, emotional, and spiritual limitations and possibilities.

By becoming aware of the children's characteristics you will be better able to provide a challenging ministry to them. In turn, they will respond in a loving appreciative manner to your genuine concern for their needs.

MIDDLERS

When Robert Raikes first started Sunday school in 1780, there was only one class—children. As Sunday schools grew, a need developed to separate and divide children according to their abilities. The first division found children in two classes, Primary and Junior. Over the years it was recognized that, because of ability-level differences, a third division was necessary. This new division was called Middlers.

The Middlers, or third and fourth graders, are unique in their interests and abilities. The problems faced in the Primary years, such as learning how to read and write, or developing muscle coordination, have subsided for the Middler.

The 8-and 9-year olds who make up your Middler class have gained confidence in their ability to do things. They can express their ideas creatively in art and in writing. They even enjoy this expression!

Middlers learn best by becoming involved in class activities. The teacher who incorporates music, drama, games, art, and a variety of other methodology, will find the Middlers responding with enthusiasm. Activities should not become an end unto themselves. The message is always more important than the method.

Activities are used to create interest in the lesson. They involve children in the discovery process. The child's retention of the lesson will increase through his active involvement. It is important therefore that all activities in the Middler class relate to, and reinforce the lesson of the day.

The use of activities and involvement comes into focus as you begin to look at the child and learn about him. Certain characteristics appear at different stages of a child's life. Even though these age-level characteristics appear about the same time in children of the same age, we must minister to children as individuals. While there are many similarities, there are also many differences in individuals.

Again, I cannot list every characteristic of the Middler child. I can, however, provide you with some generalities and specifics that will help you in the classroom.

Physical Characteristics

Physical characteristics are those things that refer to the development of the body. These include muscle coordination, abilities to do certain tasks, growth, health, and general well-being. As in the Primary area, we will only discuss those physical characteristics that relate to the Sunday school.

There are physical characteristics that are common to 8-and 9-year olds. Middlers need to move. These children are still growing and muscles that sit dormant will cramp or ache. Plan movement into every lesson.

The Middler is also full of energy. He seems to have an unlimited reserve of energy. Many teachers of Middlers would describe them as hyperactive. Although there are few medically hyperactive children, the 8-or 9-year old child could cause you to believe differently.

Mental Characteristics

The Middler is increasingly creative. Gone are the problems of learning to read, limited muscle coordination, and the social fear of not being accepted. The Middler has a short attention span. As a general rule, a child can concentrate on something about 1 minute for every year of age. While this is approximate, it does say to the teacher, "You need to keep things relatively short."

Children in the Middler age-group are curious. They want to explore and examine the world around them. Middlers will touch, play with, and take apart, anything you bring to class. Use this natural curiosity to spark interest in your lessons.

Middlers still have limited concepts of time and distance. Their recognition of these areas is becoming more developed as they read and associate themselves with other people. These associations stimulate the development of a Middler's sense of imagination. Short dramas, skits, and plays are activities Middlers enjoy. Involving Middlers in the lesson will serve to diminish discipline problems.

Most Middlers do not have an extensive vocabulary. You will find that they use many words, oftentimes without understanding. Often because they do not understand a particular word, they will substitute something that sounds close to it. This "sound alike" can lead to much misunderstanding.

As you teach the Middler, ask questions. Make sure the class understands what you are saying. Give the student opportunity to explain his ideas.

Words with symbolic meanings are another vocabulary problem. "Asking Jesus to come into your heart" can create various pictures in the minds of children. Be certain you adequately explain terms and the meanings of religious expressions and symbolism.

Middlers have been exposed to much through television and radio. Many children in the Middler age-group watch upwards of 3 and 4 hours of television each day. Acts of violence, adult situations, and vocabulary are all presented without regard to age-level or understanding. The partial understanding of information received causes confusion, fear, and misunderstandings.

Social Characteristics

Have you ever given thought to how much you've progressed socially since you were born? When the Middler was born, he was the center of his world. Gradually Mom and Dad came into his circle of friendships mainly because they met his needs of food, love, shelter, and protection.

Brothers and sisters were next as the young child's world grew. Then came relatives. Soon there were playmates. Not many, but a few. Then came preschool or kindergarten and the young child began to become acquainted with other people. In the first-grade friendships didn't come easily because for a 6-year-old there are so many new things to be involved in.

Now the Middler has become a social being. He needs the recognition of friends and adults.

Friends play an important role in the well-being of the Middler. It is important for the self-esteem of the child that classmates accept him. Each child in your Middler class wants to be accepted by the group. It is the teacher's responsibility to control behavior so that no child is picked on.

Middlers have a strong sense of fairness and justice. For the teacher, this means that how you treat each member will be watched and evaluated by the others. Help the Middler learn what the Bible says about treating others fairly and justly. You will also need to show them that God is fair and just in what He does and says.

Middlers are sensitive. Avoid criticizing them in front of their peers. Instead, take the disruptive child aside and privately discuss the offensive behavior. Never embarrass a child in front of his classmates. Jesus set the example for us in continuously lifting problem students out of their sin and hurt.

Jesus could have looked up at Zacchaeus (Luke 19) and called him names, degraded him, and embarrassed him in front of the town. Instead "When Jesus reached the spot, he looked up and said to him, 'Zacchaeus, come down immediately. I must stay at your house today'" (Luke 19:5).

Make an effort to "honestly" compliment children for their involvement and good behavior. Encourage children to accept each other and to reach out to visitors in the class.

Emotional Characteristics

Emotional traits are difficult to discover. It is only after observation that one is able to recognize them. Like other characteristics, once recognized, the teacher can apply what he knows in his approach to teaching.

Children face many pressures these days. Pressure to succeed, to be the best in sports or academics, to wear the right clothing, to have a boyfriend or a girlfriend, or to act like an adult. Many children are living in a family of divorce and still others have become part of the growing force of latch-key children. You must show acceptance and understanding to each child you serve. Accepting a child as he is goes a long way toward that child's acceptance of God's love.

Middlers need assurance from adults that they are doing the right things. When children make mistakes, they need to know that the teacher loves them and everything is going to be okay. Be sensitive to the individual and his needs. Demonstrate positive actions that show love and concern for each child.

Middlers complain a lot. This is due largely to the fact that they are idealistic and are searching for answers from their world. In class, the teacher needs to encourage the children to begin a daily series of Bible reading and study.

Explain why things are done in class and explain the rules of your class. This will help children feel at ease and secure in your class. It will also serve as a beginning of answers to the questions they may have.

The Middler can be a worrier. He worries about his homelife, pleasing the teacher, and completing work satisfactorily. Do what you can to provide age-level appropriate work that each child can succeed in accomplishing. Give them time to complete each task. By this you will be helping the child do his best work.

Compliment the child when he does well on assigned tasks. Also tell him the truth when he has not completed an activity to the best of his ability. You can assist the child in setting realistic goals for his work in and out of your class.

A Middler can become so absorbed in work that oftentimes he will lose track of his surroundings. Dedicated perfectionism is one way to describe the accomplishments of the 8-and 9-year old.

Spiritual Characteristics

The church is in existence to nurture people's spiritual being. Middlers are people who have need of such nurture. It is sometimes difficult in the group setting to ascertain a child's spiritual growth. Spend time getting to know the children and their spiritual condition. Observe appearances and rely on the Holy Spirit for guidance and wisdom. The following observations are made concerning children who have had some exposure to the church setting.

The Middler years mark the beginning of a sense of spiritual awareness for children. Although children can accept Christ as Savior at an earlier age-level, Middlers are by far the easiest age-group in which teachers can lead individuals to Christ.

The teacher should take advantage of this characteristic and give regular opportunity for children to come to Christ. Helps for leading a child to Christ are included in every quarterly of Radiant Life Curriculum.

The Middler has a good memory and is eager to learn about God. You can encourage him to study God's Word. Doctrine is introduced more formally to children of this age. The Bible Fact Pak (basis of Junior Bible Quiz) is a handy help to have for quiz games in the classroom. The 576 questions contained in the Fact Pak cover basic facts about the Bible and Pentecostal doctrine.

Middlers trust God. They believe He loves and cares for them. They enjoy listening to Bible stories and will take an active part in discussions about the Bible.

Involve children in activities that will strengthen their faith and commitment to Jesus. Prayer and Scripture reading should be a regular part of every class session. Children at this age are compassionate in their prayer for others needs.

Middlers ask questions about everything. Simple understandable answers should be given. Explanations of terminology should be available as questions arise. Eight-and nine-year olds are beginning to understand some of the abstract concepts of scripture. Love, peace, and joy begin to have meaning to the Middler.

Teaching Middlers can be the most rewarding aspect of your Christian walk. Involving them in class, fielding their questions, listening to their observations, and letting them come to Jesus will change your life. From time to time you will want to review the characteristics listed on the Middler charts. Apply these to your preparation time and presentation of the gospel.

JUNIORS

What do you do with people who are too old to be called children and too young to be called teens? You call them Juniors, give them the most creative teacher in the elementary department, and pray a lot!

The Junior is at an in-between stage in his development. He is too old and mature to want to do the things younger children do. At the same time, he is too young and immature to be involved in teen activities. One day he will enjoy childish games. The next day, he will scoff at the very same games.

Juniors are "DOERS," The Junior likes to do all sorts of things. He can get so wrapped up in doing that he totally ignores his environment. The Junior has learned to conserve his energy and can be active for longer periods of time.

Since Juniors are active they tend to get themselves into a lot of trouble. Teachers of fifth- and sixth-graders in public schools tend to report more behavioral problems among their students than teachers of other grades.

The child in his fifth-or sixth- grade year reaches his creative peak. Do not let this scare you. Because fifth-and sixth-graders are capable of understanding and applying abstract concepts, they respond well to the moving of the Holy Spirit in the classroom.

Your greatest task as a teacher of Juniors is discovering what motivates these children. If you can get them interested in what you are teaching, you will have no problem maintaining discipline.

Someone once said the joys of working with Juniors are that they are

■ Old enough to be mature.

■ Smart enough to read well.

■ Curious enough to want to learn.

■ Young enough to be impressionable.

■ Idealistic enough to want to learn the right things.

■ Ready to accept Christ and to live for Him.

For a teacher of Juniors to really succeed with his class, he must learn who Juniors are. It is not enough to come into class on Sunday morning, teach for 1 hour and never become involved with students during the week. Juniors are looking for someone to pattern their lives after. Your sincere and consistent care for them will be noticed and elicit a positive response.

Knowing a child by name does not mean that you know the child. To understand why a child acts the way he does you must know him personally. Begin by studying the characteristics for the age-level. Not every child will exhibit every characteristic. Some will show characteristics that fall above or below the norm. This does not mean that they are advanced or retarded. Every child is growing at a different rate. Do all you can to discover where each individual is and meet him there.

You will want to read this chapter, spend time getting to know your students, and apply what you have learned to your lesson preparation. Take time now to read and study the characteristics of Juniors.

Physical Characteristics

Physical characteristics are those things that deal with a Junior's physical being. They include things such as size, weight, height, health, coordination, growth, and general well-being. Only characteristics that apply to Sunday school will be discussed.

As has already been mentioned, the Junior is a doer. Because of his desire to do as many things as possible, he will at times become overextended. He must then choose which activity to do first. This should be expected and the teacher should help the Junior realize how to limit himself. This is also a good time to introduce the concept of setting priorities.

The Junior age is one of the healthiest times in a person's life. Barring out of town trips and vacations, the Junior will be a regular attender. Prepare for good attendance. Make sure you have adequate materials for every child. Take note that some children of divorce will attend only as often as the home situation allows. For instance, a child may stay with his mother two Sundays a month. On these days he attends your class. The other Sundays he does not and cannot because of distance or family preferences. Do not penalize such a child. His faithful attendance on the days he can come should be recognized and rewarded.

You can increase the length of time spent teaching the lesson and working on activities. The Junior can physically sit still for longer periods of time than Primary or Middler children. He has learned to give more attention to the teacher and is learning to pace himself.

Juniors are entering another period of radical change. Girls are maturing physically ahead of the boys. This causes some self-consciousness on the girl's part. Be sensitive to this. Physical change is beginning in the boys as well.

Because of this change, Juniors will play hard then complain of being tired. Provide physical activity followed by calm periods.

I use table or reading activities to slow them down and give them time to recharge.

Eleven-year-old boys are more restless than girls. This can be mistaken for lack of self-control. Give them movement and allow them to actively participate in every aspect of your lesson.

Mental Characteristics

The Junior years are some of the most creative times a person enjoys in his life. He is mentally alert. The Junior is developing ideals, and ready to take on almost anything. The interested Sunday school teacher can make a lasting impression on the Junior.

In studying the mental characteristics of the Junior we are not talking about his intelligence, but we are looking at his ability to perform tasks.

The Junior has a good imagination. He likes to take part in activities that show what he can do. Juniors are creative and enjoy problem-solving. Provide opportunities for the children to express their creativity. Things such as writing plays or puppet shows give the Junior a means of self-expression.

A Junior likes to read. The Junior will probably do more free time reading during these years than at any other time in his life. Free time reading is defined as reading books that are of interest to him and not on assigned topics. Mysteries, adventures, and stories of heroes are among some of the books he reads.

Take advantage of this ability and interest in reading. Some churches provide Christian books for the children to read. Keep your library of Christian books accessible to the Juniors and constantly updated.

Get a Junior interested in something. Challenge him to do it and he will give all of his time to the task. Junior Bible Quiz is an example of this. Some children are motivated to study the *Bible Fact Pak* (available from Gospel Publishing House) questions for hours.

Juniors also like to plan what they are going to do. Since they are trustworthy and responsible, allow them to take part in planning your class from time to time. They can also take part in planning class socials or outings.

These are the golden years for teaching ideas and ideals. Ten- and eleven-year-olds are looking for the ideal. They need heroes. Christ can become a hero to these children. You can become a modern-day model of the Christian ideal for the children of your class. They are looking to you as an example of faith and practice.

Juniors need adult acceptance and reassurance. Determine to build up the self-esteem of these children through positive and uplifting comments. Take time to get to know each child.

Social Characteristics

Social characteristics of a Junior deal with his relationships with others. How does he respond to his peers? Does he join in discussions with the class? Can he reach beyond his comfort zone and make new friends?

Relationships with others are very important to the Junior. A mother once approached me and told of her sixth-grade daughter. It was the family's third Sunday visiting our church. On the first Sunday a girl sat by and talked with her daughter, but asked the newcomer to move when other friends arrived. The second Sunday, this new girl sat alone during Sunday school while no one acknowledged her presence. Now on their third visit to the church, this Junior girl did not want to go to Sunday school.

Find ways to include every child in the class experience. Discussions, dramas, class outings, or gatherings should include the shy quiet child as well as the extrovert.

Because of peer pressure, a desire to belong, and curiosity, it is in the Junior years that many kids begin to experiment with smoking, drugs, and alcohol. Teacher, tune in to the needs and pressures of your Junior pupils. The answers you give must be acceptable and applicable to the Junior's life.

Juniors are very sociable. They tend to form groups (cliques). A child left out of the clique may become withdrawn or silent around the others. See to it that every child has opportunity to participate. Rearrange seating so that cliques must split up or open up themselves to others.

Find ways for the quiet child to express himself in class.

Holding visuals or participating in dramas or role-plays can help a child overcome his fears.

The Junior has a keen sense of justice. He knows what is and is not fair. Treat each class member with equal justice. It is not right for one to be punished while another is ignored for the same behavior. Fairness and justice also mean keeping your word. Promises to the class must be kept.

The Junior is torn between the peer group and the family. He is trying to determine which is most important. As a neutral party you can let the Junior know that it is all right for both to have importance in his life.

He has an increasing awareness of social problems and a growing desire to do something about them.

Competition is becoming all-important to the Junior. A Junior will compete to gain recognition for himself. Take advantage of his competitiveness and help teach him the rights and wrongs of competition. Junior Bible Quiz is excellent in its approach to competition and learning biblical knowledge.

Emotional Characteristics

Emotional characteristics cannot be seen. Fortunately, the results can be observed. Changes are taking place inside the Junior that cause him to become moody one moment and calm the next.

The Junior is prone to complaining. There are times when everything he is asked to do will be met with several reasons why he can't or doesn't want to do it. At times he will complain he is being picked on or singled out in a negative way.

While he sometimes complains, the Junior can become totally absorbed in what he is doing. When so absorbed, he may not hear a question or may consider your interruption an unnecessary distraction. He can leave a task and return to finish it.

Do all you can to involve the Junior in your lesson. Trusting him with a part of the lesson is an emotional lift. The Junior can make good choices. When involving him, give him a choice of activities. Complaints of not liking what is happening diminish if he is allowed to choose. A choice of projects and activities allows for the differing interests of your students.

Where the 10-year-old is typically cooperative, content, and easygoing, the 11-year-old questions, is restless, and will sometimes test your patience. Acceptance is one of your key tools in dealing with the Junior.

A Junior is sometimes critical of himself. When he fails to reach a goal, he becomes disappointed. Reassure him that all is not lost when he fails to achieve his goal the first time. He may set higher standards for himself, and others, than are possible to reach. This idealism is not bad but can lead to regular disappointments. Understanding and reassurance will take you a long way with the Junior.

Spiritual Characteristics

Spiritual characteristics are probably in the forefront of your thinking. You will play a major role in the child's spiritual growth. The children you serve will be operating on differing levels spiritually. Some have just come to church and been saved, while others have lived in church and for Christ almost since birth.

The Junior age is perhaps the greatest period for conversions. Provide opportunities for children to come to Christ in your class. Set a goal for the spiritual rebirth of every class member. Talk to them of salvation in and out of class.

In addition to finding Christ as his personal Savior, a Junior may be ready to receive the baptism in the Holy Spirit. If he receives no instruction in the home, then the responsibility of training falls on the church and its workers.

Every Junior needs the power that the baptism in the Holy Spirit will give him. When teaching on this subject, keep the message simple. Use the Bible to show references and explain the responsibilities expected of the believer by the Holy Spirit.

The Junior needs to belong. It is important that he feel the church is not just mom or dads church, but that it is his church as well. Many juniors have never been a part of the adult worship service. Invite your pastor and other church leaders to class outings. Work to develop a respect for the church building and for the leaders God has given your congregation.

Juniors generally have a great capacity to memorize and recall what has been learned. Provide them with good biblical material. Set challenging memory goals for them.

You will find that the Junior asks searching questions. He wants to believe, but the media, schools, and even his peer group cause him to have doubts. Take a genuine interest in questions and doubts. Use the Bible as your source for answering all the questions of life.

Ten-and eleven-year-olds are looking for heroes. Jesus can be the number one hero in every boy and girl's life. Direct the attention of the Juniors to Christ and other biblical heroes.

Instruct the Junior that God will guide and direct his entire life. It is not enough to go through the motions of accepting Christ. Jesus wants to be Lord of all. When struggles come, Jesus is there to help. When peer pressure is overwhelming, Jesus will stand by his side. God will provide the still small voice of the Holy Spirit to reveal His will in the life of each boy and girl.

This ends the section dealing with characteristics of elementary children. Study those that deal with the age-level you teach. For quick reference of these look in the Appendix at the back of this book. Pray that God will help you to apply what you know about these characteristics as you prepare your lesson each week.

How Can I Plan Powerful Lessons? 5

You can have a powerful, life changing presentation this week. Jesus wants to move in the lives of boys and girls. He said, "let the little children come to me...", and the order was never rescinded. Children can be saved in the Sunday school. Children can be filled with the Holy Spirit in the Sunday school room. Children can experience God's presence and prayers can be answered in the Sunday school room.

> "When Jesus had finished saying these things, the crowds were amazed at his teaching, because he taught as one who had authority, and not as their teachers of the law" (Matthew 7:28–29).

You can teach as Jesus taught! With God's help you can teach as one having authority. You can stand in your classroom this week, and teach under the anointing of the Holy Spirit. Your lesson can come to life in the hearts of the boys and girls. The children you teach will become more like Jesus. All of this can happen. CAUTION: The move of God I am talking about will not occur without proper preparation.

A teacher named Alice came to me. She had prayed and fasted for her class that week. Alice had meditated on God's Word as it related to her lesson. When class time came, she was ready. The lesson was presented, prayer offered, and every child in Alice's class was filled with the Holy Spirit.

Alice's class is not an isolated incident. All across our country God is moving in elementary Sunday school rooms. Faithful teachers are preparing their lessons and their hearts, and God is bringing the increase. One pastor wrote to me saying, "I was invited to speak to a class of Juniors concerning the baptism in the Holy Spirit. The morning of the class, I was detained in the hallway of our church. When I finally arrived in class, every child was kneeling. Some with hands raised and tears flowing were speaking in tongues." God had visited Sunday school before the pastor could arrive!

I am sure that your desire is to experience this kind of spiritual happening in your own Sunday school room. You may wonder, "How can I plan powerful lessons?" Implement the suggestions on the following pages as you continue in your teaching. Trust God with your Sunday school class. Now take time to read Ezra 7:10 in the King James Version.

FOLLOWING EZRA'S EXAMPLE

"For Ezra had prepared his heart to seek the law of the Lord, and to do it, and to teach in Israel statutes and judgements" (Ezra 7:10 KJV).

Time out! Make yourself a peanut butter and jelly sandwich right now. Be sure to use fresh bread, thick peanut butter, and your favorite jelly. I'll wait while you do this.

Done already? Boy, you are a fast order chef! Now while you are enjoying that sandwich, let's break Ezra 7:10 into four parts. The first thing you used in making your sandwich was a knife. It is tough to spread that peanut butter and jelly without a knife. Prayer is the knife that will spread God's blessings on your preparation. Prayer cuts through the distractions of this world and touches God's heart.

The bread of preparation is needed to hold your lesson together. Without bread, you are left with a hand full of peanut butter and jelly. What a mess! It has been said, "If you don't plan your lesson, the children will plan it for you." A powerful spiritual lesson must rest on a bed of consistent preparation.

The jelly on your sandwich represents practice. The sweetest part of teaching must be to live your lesson. Practice what you are teaching and the children will catch the message and live it themselves.

The final ingredient needed is the peanut butter. Your peanut butter is the lesson that will stick with the student. A lesson that has been put together with prayer, preparation, and practice will produce power in your pupils. Truth and experience will penetrate the barrier of sin that entraps so many children.

Now that you've eaten your sandwich, you may need a drink of cool water. That water is like the blessings of God's Spirit that will be felt in your Sunday school as you plan properly.

Pray

"Ezra had prepared his heart. . ." The preparation of the heart can only be accomplished through prayer. The good soil of a heart is cultivated by regular communication with God.

The modern Pentecostal (Charismatic) movement had its humble beginnings in a prayer meeting. We believe in storming the throne room of God with our petitions. God hears and answers prayer. Prayer for the lost, for each other, and for our ministers has always been a vital part of our heritage.

A wise teacher will spend time before God every day. Pray for the students, for the anointing of God's power on your ministry, and for other church ministries.

Pray for the Students

Get in the good habit of praying for your students each day. Keep a copy of your class roll handy and pray for every child by name. This does not have to be a lengthy time of intercession. Develop a prayer ritual in which every boy and girl is mentioned before God. Spend extra time praying for those with personal problems. Concentrate prayer for unruly or disruptive students.

You may want to post your roster on the refrigerator or on the dashboard of your car. Keep the names and the need to pray before you.

Pray for the Anointing

Pray that God would endue you with power to teach. God wants every boy and girl to be saved and to come to the knowledge of His truth. You need the fresh anointing every time you stand to teach. Do not settle for a routine of dry and unexciting Sunday school time. Turn to Jesus for power and wisdom in your teaching.

Pray for Other Ministries

You are not alone! Other ministries and lay ministers in your church need prayer. Pray for the early childhood and youth leaders. Pray for the ushers and pastors. Don't complain about other ministries. Pray for them! One of the great joys of service is found in supporting others who serve.

Prepare

"Ezra had prepared his heart to seek the law of the Lord. . ." After prayer has prepared the soil of your heart, faithful preparation must prepare the lesson you will teach.

Ezra sought the law of the Lord. He studied his lesson. To seek denotes a bit more than scanning the material on Saturday night. This suggests that the teacher should study to show himself approved; A workman that need not be ashamed. If Jesus sat in your class this week, would you be ashamed of your lack of preparation?

Good Curriculum

Good preparation begins with a good curriculum. Radiant Life is the finest Pentecostal/Full Gospel curriculum on today's market. It's presentation and methodology are up-to-date and its doctrine is sound. It is adaptable to any size group. I want my children to be firmly grounded in the full gospel message. Radiant Life is the beginning of this.

A good curriculum, however, does not contain a message for your children. Curriculum is a recipe card. It provides a systematic balanced diet of doctrinal truth. Remember, meat and potatoes can be served in many ways.

A recipe card is not the finished product. Do not stand and read the curriculum word for word to your class. You would never invite the pastor for Sunday dinner and feed him recipe cards. How can the child taste and see that the Lord is good if his teacher only provides recipe cards?

You are the Master's chef. God has given you insights, abilities, and talents that will accent what curriculum writers have put to paper. You can add to the lesson and no curses will come on you. A message from God comes as you study the curriculum, meditate on God's Word as it relates to the curriculum, and pray for the anointing.

A Little Each Day Keeps the Burn-Out Away!

Take some time every day to pray and study your lesson. Preparation begins at the end of this week's class. Do something right now. Turn the page of this book. That's how easy it is to start next week's lesson. While you are still in the classroom, turn the page. Take a look at what is coming up. Check out the theme, object, and key Scripture passage for next week.

Now on Sunday afternoon, write these down on a 3 by 5-inch card. Place this 3 by 5-inch card where it will be seen throughout the week. Each time you see it, study the verse, think about the theme, and pray that God's objective will be accomplished this week. As God gives you creative ideas, write them down on the card.

Each day spend some time working on your lesson. One teacher I know spends 15 minutes each morning before breakfast working on his lesson. On Thursday or Friday, you will want to compile all ideas and insights for your lesson. Look at available methodology and make decisions on what to use in your class. A friend of mine created a chart like the following:

Week	Bible-Story Method	Memory-Verse Method
1		
2		
3		
4		
5		

Every lesson will have a Bible story and a memory verse. Many teachers find it a struggle deciding which method to employ each week. As I have done on the first week, fill in a method that you are comfortable using to teach the Bible story and verse. Choose five different methods to put in the blanks for weeks one through five under each category.

Now take out your calendar for this year. On the first Sunday of each month write in your two methods. Do the same on the second, third, etc. You now know which method to use when teaching the Bible story and memory verse every Sunday this year. As the curriculum introduces new methods or you learn some new methods, insert these as you wish. I have found this chart helpful, and I hope you will too.

There are other short cuts I am sure you have found in your preparation. However you accomplish this task, you and I both know it takes time and work to plan a lesson. Give yourself that time this week. Be like Ezra. He sought the law of the Lord.

Practice

Ezra was a doer of God's Word. Before he ever stepped into the classroom setting, he practiced what he would teach. A good Sunday school teacher is one that sets an example in life. It is true that actions speak louder than words.

God will give you opportunities day by day to live your

upcoming lesson. One week I was going to teach about life, and life more abundantly. Driving down the interstate on Saturday, my van blew a tire. I pulled off the road and with my lesson in mind, made changing the tire an exercise in praise. My kids helped and the chore was turned to joy. The next day in class, I could speak from experience that life abundantly breaks through any problem.

Role Model

The man who hears God's Word and does it is like one who builds his house upon a rock. The storms of life will beat against it, but it will not fall. The teacher who hears God's Word and does it is building his class on the rock of godly experience. Children's lives will be touched in such a place.

Children in our nation today need heroes. You can be a hero. You can have a life-long lasting influence on a child. Your godly example will affect change. Unlike the superhero of comic book fame, you will make mistakes. Part of the discipleship process is handling such mistakes. Children will be witness to your humanity. They will see how you handle the trials and the triumphs and will follow your example.

Think back to a teacher that affected you in a positive way. That man or woman influenced your manner of living. The way you teach is a partial reflection of that teacher's good work.

Life Application

Some of the best lessons are those born in curriculum and raised to readiness in the neighborhood of life experience. Practicing a lesson is such a practical habit to obtain. Each day, God will reveal new and wonderful insights for this week's class. Pray that the Holy Spirit will bring to remembrance those life experiences that will best represent the lesson.

Kids love to hear stories about teachers' childhoods. Almost weekly some memory is stirred about my elementary years. Be careful to tell those stories that will point children toward the cross. Old horror stories of your sinning years should be avoided.

If this week's lesson is on divine healing then pray for the sick.

If you are teaching about witnessing then go out and witness. Nothing can compare to a fresh testimony for getting kids excited about Jesus. A genuine life experience injected with God's power teaches much better than a word for word reading of curriculum.

Children are impressed by the truth. Like adults, they are moved by testimony. Overcome the influence of the world this week by the Word of God and the word of your testimony.

Present

Ezra prayed, prepared, and practiced his lesson. Only after he was fully ready did he step into the arena of the classroom. Can you imagine an Olympic athlete stepping up to the line for a race with little or no preparation? Of course not! The athlete spends many hours day after day training for the race. He goes over his every move again and again in his mind until that race is part of his very being. And all this for a race that may last less than 11 seconds. Teacher, your faithfulness in praying, preparing, and practicing will have eternal impact as you present your lesson.

Creativity

You are a creative person! God has given you creativity. You have different talent and abilities than I have. That is the way God planned it. You are an individual with creativity and talents that are tailor-made for the students in your class, your church, and your community.

The lesson you teach this Sunday will be unique. I could give one hundred Middler teachers the same curriculum and materials, put them in like classrooms with equal attendance, and every lesson will be different.

God has given every teacher the same amount of preparation time. He has given every teacher creativity, the Bible, and the Holy Spirit. Trust in God for the words to say as you present this week's lesson.

The presentation includes many parts. The following is a sample schedule/lesson plan of an average elementary Sunday school class.

Sunday Schedule

- ■ 9:00 Teacher arrives and begins setting up the room, visuals, etc.
- ■ 9:07 Students arriving. Teacher talks with and listens to the students, allows them to assist in any further set-up, and begins presession activity. Roll is taken.
- ■ 9:30 Teacher opens in prayer and the lesson begins.
- ■ Song(s)
- ■ Memory verse
- ■ Object lesson
- ■ Bible story
- ■ Bible-learning activity
- ■ Life-application story
- ■ Prayer/Response time
- ■ Quiz Game
- ■ 10:30 Class is dismissed with prayer. Teacher again talks with, and listens to children. Any mess is cleaned up. Teacher looks at curriculum and begins thinking about next week's lesson.

Notice the class opens and closes with prayer. Everything in class should lead to a time of response. This response time must occur before any warning bell is sounded. You and I both know that when the 2-minute warning sounds, your class checks out of the game. The children may remain in their seats physically but you have lost them mentally.

The following are some methods that can be utilized in the class presentation.

> Music, games, puppetry, object lessons, Scripture pictures, storytelling, video, crafts, puzzles, flannelgraph, cartooning, balloons, drama, role-play, discussion, overhead, testimonies, audio recordings, modern parables, costumed characters, juggling, and chalk-talks.

You can experience God's power in your class this week. Jesus taught as one having authority. With proper prayer, preparation, and practice, your presentation will be wonderful. So prepare and teach a powerful presentation.

What Motivates Elementary Children?

6

> The Teacher searched to find just the right
> words, and what he wrote was upright and
> true (Ecclesiastes 12:10).

I sn't this the key to all great teaching? A teacher must find just the right words and just the right way to say them. I once heard a pastor say, "Einstein said that 98 percent of education is motivation." Whether the statistic is true or not makes little difference. The fact remains that if a teacher can discover what motivates his students, and apply that to his words and activities in the classroom, then children will learn.

What is it that motivates elementary children? Is it possible to have a well-ordered elementary class without offering a 3-foot candy bar, a ride on a fire truck, or a trip to the lake? Both questions will be answered in this chapter. Children in our age of high-tech hype can and will be motivated in a nonjudgemental environment of discovery.

THE ABCS OF MOTIVATION

Acceptance

Children need an environment of unconditional acceptance. The foul mouthed, dirty clothed kid deserves the same attention as the pretty little deacon's daughter who always has the answers.

Bible

God's Word is a great motivator. Helping a child hide Scripture in his heart is perhaps your greatest service as a teacher. The Holy Spirit will bring Scripture passages to a child's remembrance again and again, motivating him to do right.

Competition

Children are motivated by competitive events, but keep competition on a friendly level. There is no room in Sunday school for contests that cause animosity. I love to provide competition in which any child who tries receives some kind of reward.

Discipline

Children love discipline. They need rules in the classroom. (This will be dealt with more fully in the next chapter.)

Environment

The room decor, odor, and arrangement has much to do with a child's motivation. If he is uncomfortable, learning becomes difficult. A well lit, bright, uncluttered classroom will excite and inspire children. Check out your environment this week.

Fellowship

Children come to Sunday school to meet with each other and to meet with God. Give them time to talk with their friends.

Greed

Children love prizes. We call these educational incentives. The world calls them bribes. Whatever term you use, there is nothing wrong with rewarding a child for a job well done. A boy or a girl may be inspired to learn a verse, to behave in class, or to help others as the result of a prize.

Happiness

Sunday school should be a happy experience. Joy must be high on your priority list. Do all you can to make class fun for the children. To a child there is nothing worse than a boring Sunday school class.

Involvement

Involved children will retain more and pay closer attention to the lesson. Trust your students with ministry tasks. Children can help set up the classroom, hand out papers, hold object lessons, or even teach their friends. Get them involved.

Justice

Boys and girls have a well-developed sense of justice. They know when the teacher plays favorites. Children are quick to remind you when something isn't fair. Pray for wisdom. God will help you to be just in your dealings with the class.

Kindness

Show kindness to the children. Your example in this area will mean much to a child. Boys and girls are hurting in this world we live in. It is rare that an adult will show kindness to children.

Listen

Listen to the children. During presession and in the halls of the church, listen to the child who speaks to you. If need be get down on his level. Maintain eye contact with the child. Pay attention! What he is saying may have eternal significance. If you really care, you will really listen.

Mission

Children need to know that Christianity is more than just sitting and learning on Sundays. Without a vision the Sunday school class perishes. Instill in children an evangelistic urgency. Sunday school is a discipleship process that prepares them to be witnesses.

Nature

Kids love animals and other natural things. Bring the wonders of God's creation into your classroom. Rock collections and live bugs motivate elementary children. Such items can serve to keep a childs' attention. Tie these to eternal truth as Jesus did with the vines and branches and the sower and the seed.

Optical Stimulation

Do not lecture the children. Give them something to look at. Children retain much more when they can see the lesson as well as hear it. This is one reason that curriculum provides visual aid.

Peer Pressure

I believe peer pressure was created by God for the good of the church. With so much negative peer pressure in the world, why not turn this motivational force around and use it in the class. For instance, memorizing Scripture can become the "in thing."

Quality

Children are impressed by quality. Quality does not have to mean big spending. Do your best to make every part of the Sunday school experience the best it can be. "Whatever you do, work at it with all your heart, as working for the Lord, not for men" (Colossians 3:23).

Recognition

Compliment a child when he does right. When a child finishes a project or memorizes a Scripture verse, recognize him in front of the class.

Security

In this divorce-torn world we live in, children are looking for a secure sanctuary of love. Your faithfulness in teaching provides children with security. Your presence in the Sunday school week after week and year after year provides a stability that children need.

Testimonies

The truth impresses children. True stories of God's goodness will motivate children toward a deeper Christian experience.

Unknown

Surprise the class once in a while. Children are very curious. They love to explore, to follow clues, and to discover previously unknown concepts. Become a tour guide into the unknown.

Variety

The same old sequence using the same old methods will inspire the same old response. The children will be bored! Variety can be the spice your classroom needs. Try something new this week. Caution: younger children should be forewarned when a new method or structure is being introduced. The Primary student thrives on structure and order while the Junior student needs a few surprises.

Words

"The wise in heart are called discerning, and pleasant words promote instruction" (Proverbs 16:21). Words carry the power to make or break a child. Use words to lift children up. Focus on good behavior and compliment the child who obeys your rules. Never approach children with condemning speech. Speak to every child in the same way you address our Savior.

Excitement

Get excited! Excitement is contagious. You are teaching about the most exciting Book ever written. Put some feeling into the lesson. Get motivated. It is hard to motivate children if you are not excited about the lesson.

You

A psychologist on a radio talk show said, "The most important and effective educational toy you can give a child is his parent." As a teacher, you are the most important and effective tool in your classroom. Your appearance, actions, words, and attitudes will motivate children to want to learn. A variety of methodology will interest children for a time, but it takes a dedicated, compassionate teacher to hold their attention week after week.

Zeal

Last, but not least, is zeal. A zeal for more of Jesus and the things of God must be evident in the elementary Sunday school. It is not enough to teach lessons out of well-ordered commitment. The teacher must have a genuine love for God. Your zealousness will be the lesson children will catch. Children need a real living Jesus and your Christian fervor will demonstrate that reality to them.

MOTIVATIONAL TYPES

Adults as well as children are typically motivated in one of two ways. Extrinsic or intrinsic motivation. Extrinsic motivation deals with external forces pushing, pulling, or inspiring a child to accomplish or to succeed. Intrinsic motivation is that power, feeling, or impulse from within that drives a child onward.

Every child is motivated by both of these at different times. My son is extrinsically/externally motivated to do the dishes. Promise of an allowance and possible pain send him back to the kitchen sink to accomplish this task. He demonstrates little or no intrinsic/internal motivation when it comes to household chores like the dishes.

This same child is intrinsically motivated to play basketball. I do not have to offer rewards or punishments to get him out front with a basketball. He loves to shoot hoops alone or in a crowd.

In the church it has always been my goal to move children from the external to the internal to the greatest motivational factor, the eternal.

Move children from the...

ETERNAL to the INTERNAL to the ETERNAL

It is not wrong to give away prizes. Prizes will motivate children to excel in Bible quiz, evangelism, and many other areas of ministry. I want the child who only completes a task for the prize to grow into deeper motivations.

A prime example of this is the kids crusade. On the average, kids crusade prizes are offered for bringing visitors. In one such crusade a girl named Sarah transported 57 different children to the church in 4 days of meetings. She won the grand prize and while up front I asked her, "Why did you bring so many people to the crusade?"

She answered, "At first I just wanted the prize, but then I saw my friends praying at the altar." Sarah had moved from the external motivation of winning the prize to the eternal motivation of the joy of seeing someone come to Christ.

Some of the children she invited came because of a promise of puppets and candy (External). Several returned on their own later in the week because of our follow-up program. Each child received a phone call and a personal visit. The personal touch caused them to want to come back even if no prize was offered (Internal). Those same children prayed at the altars, received Christ, and returned to our children's church on Sundays (Eternal).

In a church in Oregon the children's pastor offered a Bible just like his to the first child to memorize the Book of James. One week later a 10-year-old girl named Gina came to church with the entire Book of James committed to memory. She memorized it to win that leather bound reference Bible, but in doing so developed a new love for God's Word. The girl continued to memorize Scripture passages after the original contest.

Discover what it is that motivates the individuals in your class. Apply this knowledge to your lesson preparation. Get motivated and the children will follow suit. Together you will reap eternal blessings in the Sunday school class.

Discipline Or Disaster?

7

"He entered the church now with a swarm of clean and noisy boys and girls, proceeded to his seat and started a quarrel with the first boy that came handy. The teacher, a grave elderly man, interfered; then turned his back a moment, and Tom pulled a boy's hair in the next bench, and was absorbed in his book when the boy turned around; stuck a pin in another boy, presently, in order to hear him say "Ouch!" and got a new reprimand from his teacher. Tom's whole class were of a pattern — restless, noisy and troublesome."

— Tom Sawyer, Mark Twain

Discipline in Sunday school hasn't changed that much in the last 100 years. Children still disrupt the planned activities. Teachers still work at maintaining control in the classroom. God still enters the Sunday school to bring peace, decency, and order.

I believe in discipline. A well-ordered class is healthy for the spiritual formation of children. Sometimes discipline turns into a disaster. Class becomes a war between the servant of God and "those" children. Oftentimes this problem occurs because children are actually punished while "true discipline" is nonexistent. There is a difference between discipline and punishment.

Punishment is a temporary answer to an eternal problem. Discipline holds an eternal answer. Punishment focuses on getting even. Discipline helps a child build a positive self-image and grow in self-control.

Punishment says, "If you do that one more time, I am going to send you to the adult service to sit by your parents." You have just taught the child that it is punishment to sit in church by his parents.

Discipline says, "I want to help you grow in love for yourself and for those around you." Discipline asks the questions, "What caused you to do that?" and, "How can you control yourself in the future?" In discipline a child is guided into a positive life-style. To discipline a child is to show Christlike tough love towards him. I love you, therefore I will give you boundaries to live within.

Children want discipline and loathe punishment. I once heard in a workshop that discipline includes instruction, correction, and encouragement.

Needed

Instruction

Correction

Encouragement

I added the "Needed" part because discipline should not be a bone-chilling process. Now isn't that N.I.C.E.? Children need and want discipline. The discipline they are taught in church will spill over into every area of their lives. The Christian life is one of discipline. Instruct the child in patient love. No finger wagging, nagging teachers in my Sunday school.

Instruct the child concerning what was done wrong and why it is important. Show the benefits of obedience as outlined in Scripture. Take this opportunity to train him up in the way he should go.

Correction is a process that turns the offender from bad to good. This may include a stiff lecture but always is laced with and including prayer. Pray with the child and allow him to pray. Correction will help the child to turn from evil to do right.

Encouragement recognizes the worth of the child in your sight and God's sight. Let him know that you believe he can follow your rules. Encourage him to be a doer of God's Word, not a hearer only. The following are some thoughts to keep in mind in the realm of discipline.

1. Never utilize corporal punishment.

Children must never be physically assaulted by anyone at church. Spanking, roughhousing, slapping, or dragging have no place in the Sunday school.

2. Develop and reinforce simple rules.

Each Sunday you will want to begin your class with a reminder of simple understandable rules. This gives you a base for discussion when discipline becomes necessary.

3. Never brag on the consequences of disobedience.

The minute you tell them what will happen if they break your rules, some boy will break one just to see if you are serious.

4. Be positive.

I tell the children each week that they can obey the rules. Proverbs 16:21 says, "The sweetness of the lips increaseth learning" (KJV). Be sweet. Positive messages from the teacher throughout a class session can greatly improve overall behavior. You might say, "I like how Dave is coloring his paper," or " I am glad that Jean is doing such a wonderful job obeying our rules."

5. Change your activity.

Perhaps you are the problem. If more than a couple of children are getting restless, shift gears and get them actively involved in the lesson.

My mother says, "If the children are busy, they don't have time to be discipline problems." Mom ought to know. She has taught elementary school since I was a third-grade class clown.

6. Remind them of your rules.

From time to time without great fanfare, restate your rules. Repetition is the key to learning.

7. Do not embarrass a child in front of his peers.

Would Jesus put down the creativity of an individual? Would He mock another for all to enjoy? I think not. Determine now to treat the children with the same respect you desire from them.

8. Walk in the child's direction.

Some eye contact and a step or two towards the child will many times cause a cease fire without a single word being uttered.

9. Put a hand on a child's shoulder.

Sometimes a hand gently placed on the shoulder will help a child with that temporary lack of self control.

10. Use the 2-week rule.

If a child disrupts your class 2 weeks in a row, then talk to his parents. You may discover a reason for this new behavior. (You may find out the parents are part of the problem.)

11. Pray for the child.

Spend time in prayer for children who become disruptive. Pray that God will surround them with His peace and give you an extra dose of compassion.

12. Be a shadow.

If a child becomes a continuing nuisance, assign an adult worker, of the same gender, to sit by him and take him out of the room when necessary. This shadow continues to teach the child and returns him to the room when peace reigns again.

13. Seat a child somewhere else.

Never return a child to the same seat after you have talked and prayed with him. Seat him somewhere else in the room so that he might not be tempted by his regular audience.

14. Visit the home whenever possible.

There is no substitute in discipline for a relationship with the child and his parents. A visit to the home will tell you much about the affects of his life-style as relative to his behavior. You learn much about a child when seeing his room at home. Begin to understand him through his everyday environment.

15. Plan more movement in the class experience.

God made children with wiggles and giggles. To attempt to force a class to sit still in one place is to work against the Manufacturer's warranty. Involve the children physically in the Sunday school experience.

The following is a summary of what I do when an individual causes continuing disruptions in my classroom.

■ *Have an encounter on an individual level.*

I want to speak personally and privately to the child who has a temporary lack of self-control. I strive never to embarrass a child in front of his peers. Take the child to the side or to the back of the room and talk with him.

■ *Explain the broken rule.*

Talk with the child about the importance of your rules and obedience to them. *enforce a restriction - isolation or removal*

■ *Encourage repentance.*

Repent means to turn around. The child can choose, with God's help, to turn from habits of disobedience and disruption to good behavior.

■ *Engage in Prayer.*

Prayer is the next logical step in this process. I always pray first. In my prayer, I ask God to help me become a better teacher. I want to model dependence on God so that child, in turn, will pray and put his trust in Jesus.

You can hold a well-ordered class. Discipline in the classroom

Final call a parent

can be a joy instead of a disaster. As with Tom Sawyer's teacher, there will be occasional disruptions that you will have to handle. Let God work in you for the discipleship of His children. Make this aspect of teaching a matter of prayer as well as a practice.

Can I Reach Children?

J esus said, "Let the little children come to me, and do not hinder them, for the kingdom of heaven belongs to such as these" (Matthew 19:14). This simple directive for the Church has never been rescinded. Jesus' command for you and me is still, "Let the little children come to me."

Reaching children is an important role of Sunday school. The Sunday school, a center of education and evangelism, provides an ideal setting for boys and girls to come to Christ. The student's relationship with a godly teacher naturally lends itself to the presentation of the gospel. The peer reinforcement towards a Christlike life-style is natural in the Sunday school class.

Before covering the mechanics of leading a child to Christ, there are some areas that need to be considered. If these are taken care of, the unchurched child will be more likely to return to your class a second and third time. He will be more likely to commit his life to Christ. If the Elementary Sunday school class is to be a center of education and evangelism for the child then these factors must be dealt with.

FIRST IMPRESSION

First impressions are lasting impressions. When a child or his parents first enter your Sunday school room, what do they see? How do they feel? What do they think? Will they return next week? Will these parents feel good about leaving their child in your room? These questions and more must be dealt with if the first impression is to be a positive one. Let's look at four P's of first impressions: Properties, People, Presence and Practics.

Properties

Walk into your classroom. Try to imagine being a first-time visitor. Is the room bright and cheerful? Are the visuals on the walls attractive? How does the room smell?

Many times, I walk into classrooms that are stuffy, dull, cluttered, and boring. The day is past when visiting parents will allow their children to sit in dark boiler rooms. Check your room. Clean it! Throw away the clutter of old take-home papers that sit on the table in the corner. Find a different place to store the sets from last year's Christmas program.

Children need space to move, to grow, and to learn. Providing a clean well-kept classroom will encourage boys and girls to come to Jesus. It will give parents a sense of confidence in the ministry that takes place in such a room. Finally, you will feel better about teaching in such an environment.

I have, from time to time, walked on my knees into the room I serve in. This gives me a child's view of my setting for success. I learned through this to place bulletin boards lower on the walls, to sit or kneel when I tell a Bible story, and to bring more color to the long-term decorations. I want my classroom to reach out visually and capture the imagination of the child.

People

You are the next item that falls under the scrutiny of visiting families. I tell my classroom team to brush their teeth, comb their hair, wear nice clean clothes, and smile! You represent Christ. You may be the only Christ this child will ever see.

Everything about the Sunday school teacher should say, "I love you and understand your level of development and I will guide you in an unforgettable way to Jesus." Nothing is worse than for a new child to meet a grumpy, unsmiling, harried person. Your calm controlled manner helps to ease the fear of entering an unknown situation.

Are the other children in your class giving a good first impression? Sarah was in the sixth grade. She took it upon herself to welcome and befriend newcomers to her church. Others followed Sarah's example and soon every guest, in the fifth and sixth grades, was made to feel a part of his class. This is not always the case among children. Many times the visitor is not acknowledged by anyone other than the teacher. Children need friends!

Work with the children in your class. Like their adult counterparts, children forget common courtesy. They rarely think about reaching beyond the comfort zone of old friendships. Encourage children to reach out to newcomers. Develop an atmosphere of friendliness in the ministry of your classroom. Every child that enters must feel welcomed by you and by their peers.

Presence

The visiting child must feel God's presence in the classroom as well as your presence in the community.

The genuine presence of Jesus Christ will do more to bring back first time visitors than gifts, hugs, or special attention given. Matthew 21 records Jesus' visit to the temple. As you read this passage, pay special attention to the role children played in this particular confrontation.

"But when the chief priests and the teachers of the law saw the wonderful things he did and the children shouting in the temple area, 'Hosanna to the Son of David,' they were indignant. 'Do you hear what these children are saying?' they asked him. 'Yes,' replied Jesus, 'have you never read, 'From the lips of children and infants you have ordained praise ?'" (Matthew 21:15, 16).

These were not children hyped to a frenzy by a Sunday school cheerleader. They had experienced the presence and power of Jesus and just naturally praised Him. Children today need to experience the presence and power of God. Judges 2:10 says, "After that whole generation had been gathered to their fathers, another generation grew up, who knew neither the Lord nor what he had done for Israel." I want to do all I can to ensure no repetition of this in the history of today's church. My desire for you is that your class will grow up knowing God and knowing the works He can do today!

PRACTICS

Try some of the following practical ideas for making a child feel welcome in your classroom.

Greeters

Assign children to serve as greeters. These greeters welcome everyone entering the classroom. New visitors are greeted, treated with respect, given name tags, and introduced to other children. The greeter makes sure each child is seated with others of like interest or gender.

Name Tags

One of the best ways to make a child feel at ease is to use his name with respect. Name tags will help you and the students learn the visitor's name. They also help the visitor to learn the names of those around him.

Trust

Trust the new child to help in class. He can serve along side of those who have been in class before. A newcomer can hand out papers, act out a part in the Bible story, or hold an object for an object lesson. When you trust a child with simple responsibility, you gain a friend. He will want to come back to the class where an adult cares.

Visitor's Packet

Many churches have put together a visitor's packet for children. The visitor's packet may include information about the children's ministries of your church, a tract, a take home paper, and a small gift. If your church does not provide such a packet, you can put one together for your individual class.

Information Sheet

Fill out a pupil information sheet immediately upon a child's first visit to your class. The pupil information sheet is a way you have of getting to know the student better. The basic information collected on this helps you to know how to assist the child in the learning process. This sheet should include the following information:

Child's Name _____

Address _____

Phone # _____

Birth Date _____

Dad's Name, Phone # _____

Mom's Name, Phone # _____

(Attach a picture of the child.)

FORWARD MOTION

Evangelism of children must continue to be a priority in the Sunday school. We have an opportunity to move forward into the harvest field of boys and girls. With this in mind we know that boys and girls do not just magically appear in the classroom. Now is the time to "go out into the roads and country lanes and compel them to come in."

Children can be reached by the Sunday school teacher. You can share Christ with a child and see a transformation by His grace. The following is a simple list of ideas for outreach which originates in your classroom.

Class Parties

Parties in the classroom on Sunday become ideal times for students to invite a friend. Likewise, in the home or in the church at other times, a party can become a great evangelism tool.

Field Trips or Outings

Taking a group of elementary children to the zoo may not seem very spiritual. Remember the admonition to parents in Deuteronomy 6:7,8 "Impress them on your children. Talk about them when you sit at home and when you walk along the road, when you lie down and when you get up. Tie them as symbols on your hands and bind them on your foreheads." This translates wonderfully in the field trip or outing.

Note: You should always involve parents and other church leaders in outings, field trips and parties. Strive for a ratio of one adult for every three or four children.

Programs

Class or cooperative programs do much to reach unchurched families. Invite parents and other family members to witness the children reciting Bible verses, singing songs, or presenting drama. The kids love to perform and the families love to participate. Programs seem to draw even the most hardened heathen to the Sunday school.

Other Ministries

Ministries such as kids crusade and Vacation Bible School are traditionally outreach efforts of the Sunday school. Do all you can to make such events a success. The Sunday school staff should be actively involved in any outreach event planned for your church.

GOAL SETTING

Talk and pray with the children in your class. Reaching others is the responsibility of every believer, young or old. Boys and girls may surprise you in their evangelistic fervor.

I set evangelism goals with the children in my class one Sunday. We prayed and class was dismissed. One week later a girl named Dafne approached me after class.

She said, "Brother Dick, I got one!"

I answered, "You got one what?"

With a huge smile on her face she announced, "I won my friend to the Lord. You see I invited her over to spend the night at my house. We listened to Christian tapes and watched Christian videos. By breakfast she wanted Jesus. So we prayed."

"That is fantastic, Dafne," I exclaimed.

She then said matter of factly, "I'm going to get another one."

Instill a vision in the hearts and lives of the children you serve. This vision for souls will drive all of you to more effective outreach. As children witness others coming to Christ, the vision will grow stronger.

REMEMBER: A goal is a specific, reachable, measurable plan of attack. How many new visitors do you want to see in your class every month? How many do you want to see saved? How many do you expect to attend a class outing?

Encourage the children to make and to keep a prayer list. Those they wish to be saved should be included on this list. Begin the list with family members, relatives, and close friends. Move to children in the neighborhood and at school. I encourage children to also pray for pastors, missionaries, and evangelists. It is important that children begin to see the big picture of nationwide and world evangelism. The call of evangelism extends from the individual child to the whole world.

RESPONSE TIME

In Orlando, Florida, a 12-year-old girl came to know Christ. It was the first time in her life that she had ever come to church. In Salem, Oregon, a Junior teacher led two boys to Jesus. These boys found new life in a response time at the end of their Sunday school class. A Middler teacher in Omaha, Nebraska prayed with her class. Every child was baptized in the Holy Spirit.

Is response time important? Yes! Can the Creator of this universe enter your room and touch the hearts and lives of boys and girls? Yes!

The classroom must become a center of evangelism. Everything you do, from the time the first child enters in your presession to the last object lesson, must lead to a time of response. Each week your class will build to a time of response where children can become doers of the Word, not hearers only.

You are training the children in the way they should go. A big part of that way is listening and responding to God. The response time should never be hurried or forced. The encouragement that you give is an act of letting the children come to Jesus. You never push or drag a child to our Savior. You let them come to Jesus in a calm, atmosphere of compassion.

Week after week as the children pray, they learn that Sunday school is a place to meet with God. They will be more likely to bring unsaved friends knowing that you will give an altar call each time you meet. Your faithfulness to this will be rewarded as you witness children coming to know Christ, praying one for another and experiencing the miraculous.

You do not have to be a pastor to lead children in prayer. As a Christian, the Holy Spirit dwells in and with you. Be sensitive in these times of response to listen to that still small voice as the Holy Spirit directs the class. You can pray for and receive healing. Children can be filled with the Holy Spirit. God will use you to produce an eternal impact on the children of your class.

Like other portions of the Sunday school hour, your response time should include variety. The same old prayer, prayed in the same old way each week will bore the students. Response in prayer can be just as exciting as the story or memory verse.

Let me remind you to take your time. Never rush an encounter with God. For this reason you may wish to begin your response time about 5 to 10 minutes before the end of class. For some this will be a few minutes before the warning bell sounds. (Some Sunday schools employ a 2 or 3 minute warning before class is over. A bell sounds and both teachers and students know class is over. Prayer after this bell is always rushed and seldom effective.)

There is something about physically moving towards a commitment to God that is valuable for a child. As he stands and moves from point A to point B, the response that he is making is better recorded in his memory. Many adults can point to a specific time when they responded physically to God by walking to the front of a classroom or church.

Whether you have 4 kids or 40, response time works. It is important always to speak in understandable terms and be as specific as possible. When entering a time of response, repeat what you are expecting of the children several times.

Music is an integral part of the traditional Pentecostal response time. In the typical service, as the Pastor begins the altar call, chords of soft worship rise from the organ. This mood music seems to help the sinner walk to the altar. You do not have to use music to experience the presence of God. Children can meet God with or without a worship song. If you wish, find a soothing worship tape to play on a recorder during your response time. Although not necessary, music can be an effective background to the response time.

I've listed below some different ways to approach your response time. Mix and match these to fit your particular setting. I try to change the response time about every other week. My goal is to create such an excitement that children will look forward to our response time.

Altar Call

An altar call is the traditional approach. Have the children close their eyes and think about the theme of the day. Sometimes I just tell them to close their eyes and think about Jesus. Those that wish to respond to today's lesson raise a hand. After the hand is raised, encourage them to stand and step to the front of the room. When up front either lead the children in a prayer or urge them to pray in their owns words or in their own way.

Altar Service

An altar service is more of a group activity. Invite the children to gather at one point in your classroom. Typically, the front of the room is used as an altar area. In the altar service, children are encouraged to worship and pray as a group. The class can kneel, stand, or even sit together. Children may even pray one for another.

Group Prayer

Divide your class into smaller groups. If you have four children, make two groups of two. In the larger class, groups of three or four is effective. Assign a location in your room for each group. Children in each group should pray one for another. Sometimes they may even hold hands and pray.

Prayer At the chair

When beginning the response time, ask the children to turn and kneel at their seats. Those wishing prayer for specific needs are asked to raise a hand. Circulate through your class praying for those with special needs.

Prayer Circle

The entire class stands and makes a circle around the room. Children may or may not hold hands in this circle. Take turns going around the circle with each person praying out loud. If a person does not know what to pray, they may pass to the next. Have them pass by speaking a key phrase such as, "I love you Jesus," or "Thank you God."

Prayer Partners

Have the children pair off with one or two friends. The prayer partners spend time sharing and praying for each other in the classroom. The children may then exchange phone numbers and call one another for special prayer throughout the week.

Written Requests

Children are given paper and pencil. Ask them to write down their specific needs. Papers may be collected and prayed over. In one church I visited, children pinned these requests on a cardboard cross in the front of the room. After requests are written out and prayed over, keep a record of the answers that God provides. You may want to begin a prayer notebook. Lists of prayers and answers can be kept and read occasionally as an encouragement to the children.

Whatever method you employ, children need a time of response. Give your class the opportunity to meet God each week. Let them come unto Jesus. Eternal changes will occur in your ministry, class, and in their lives.

Can you reach children? The answer is yes! God has called you and will equip you to reach boys and girls for Him. Commit your ministry in and out of the classroom to one of reaching lost children with the good news of God's love.

What About The Holy Spirit?

9

Elementary children need the baptism in the Holy Spirit. This experience is not only part of our Pentecostal heritage, but it is vital to the survival of today's believer. Sin abounds in the world in which we live. Children are being bombarded with images, words, and temptations that seek to destroy them. God gives believers His Holy Spirit to guide them into all truth, to remind them of what they have learned in Sunday school and church, and to empower them for ministry.

The baptism in the Holy Spirit is a baptism of power. The Holy Spirit dwells in and with every boy and girl who has accepted Christ.

Jesus said, "For John baptized with water, but in a few days you will be baptized with the Holy Spirit" (Acts 1:5). The baptism in the Holy Spirit is a second wonderful experience that every Christian, young or old, should desire.

More than a decade ago, I sat as my friend, the Reverend Don Meyer, preached a wonderful sermon on the Holy Spirit baptism. That sermon included seven things that the baptism in the Holy Spirit is not. I have adapted and used this material effectively with children since that time. In a majority of cases children who have heard these points explained have desired and received the Holy Spirit.

7 Things the Baptism In the Holy Spirit Is Not

1. It is not the same as salvation (Acts 19:1–6).
2. It is not just for Bible times (Acts 2:39).
3. It is not for adults only (Acts 2:17, 2:39, 21:5).
4. It is not scary (1 John 4:16 & 18).
5. It is not an experience where tongues are optional (Acts 2:4;19:6).
6. It is not an end (Acts 2).
7. It is not natural (Acts 2:4).

1. The baptism in the Holy Spirit is not the same as salvation.

In Acts chapter 19:1–7, we read of Paul's encounter with a group of believers in Ephesus. The believers had been baptized in John's baptism. They stated, "We have not even heard that there is a Holy Spirit." Paul explained salvation through Christ to these men. They accepted the message, were baptized in Jesus' name, and then Paul placed his hands on them and prayed. Every man was then filled with the Holy Spirit. Two separate experiences are mentioned in this chapter. The Ephesians believed on the Lord Jesus, (salvation), and then were empowered for ministry, (Holy Spirit).

2. The baptism in the Holy Spirit is not just for Bible times.

Men and women and boys and girls throughout church history have received this infilling. On the day of Pentecost, Peter said, "The promise is for you and your children and for all who are far off—for all whom the Lord our God will call" (Acts 2:39). Children are being filled with the Holy Spirit today! God is no respecter of persons whether by race, gender, or age. He is the same yesterday, today, and forever. This experience is for today's church.

3. The baptism in the Holy Spirit is not for adults only.

God's promises are for every believer. I know that a child may not understand all of the theological or eternal implications of speaking in tongues. I don't understand all of them either! I know that even though many things in this life are reserved for adults, God gives freely of His Spirit to those who seek Him regardless of their age. The Pentecostal/Charismatic promises of Scripture that we cling to are never prefaced by a child-exclusion clause. God wants to and will fill boys and girls with His Spirit.

4. The baptism in the Holy Spirit is not scary.

God will never do anything to harm or to scare His children. Boys and girls often wonder if God is going to move their lips uncontrollably. This is a scary proposition for a child of any age. God will not move a child's lips. He will not scare a child who sincerely seeks Him. John wrote, "And so we know and rely on the love God has for us. God is love. Whoever lives in love lives in God, and God in him. In this way, love is made complete among us so that we will have confidence on the day of judgment, because in this world we are like him. There is no fear in love. But perfect love drives out fear, because fear has to do with punishment. The one who fears is not made perfect in love" (1 John 4:16–18).

In many altar times, I have prayed with children who just couldn't seem to break through to God. When counseling with them, I have found that fear of the unknown has stood as a wall between them and God's power. His perfect love can drive out this fear. When the fear is gone, the child will receive.

5. The baptism in the Holy Spirit is not an experience where tongues are optional.

There are so many options in this life. A boy buying a skateboard can choose between literally dozens of wheels. His board can be painted and shaped a hundred different ways. One thing is not optional though. When he buys a skateboard, there will be a board and there will be wheels. Without a board and wheels, it just isn't a skateboard.

When you are filled with the Holy Spirit, you will speak with other tongues. This is not an option. It will happen. It happened in Bible times and it still happens today. The prayer language you receive is a sign that the empowerment has taken place.

Help the child understand that God gives us the words to say and that we simply open our mouths and say them. I have never witnessed a child being filled with the Spirit who had his mouth shut. In every case, children who actively, vocally praise God are the ones who receive this gift. Because of this, I encourage children to ask God for this gift and then to praise Him.

7. The baptism in the Holy Spirit is not an end.

This experience is a beginning for the believer. It is a beginning of a life of victory over sin. He is empowered to witness! Many children, after receiving the Holy Spirit, will brag to others, "I've got it!" I have even seen children sitting back during an altar time, as if to say, "I received that gift last year, I don't have to pray any more." Help children to realize that the Christian, even after he receives the Holy Spirit, should seek God's face on a daily basis. The baptism in the Holy Spirit is not an end. It is a beginning!

8. The baptism in the Holy Spirit is not natural.

This is a supernatural gift. "All of them were filled with the Holy Spirit and began to speak in other tongues as the Spirit enabled them" (Acts 2:4). The Spirit gives us the words to say. This is supernatural. Neither you nor I can teach a child how to speak in tongues. God is more than able to give children the words to say. They do not need a vocal jump start for this supernatural experience.

I often liken the use of this newly received gift to that of a new bicycle. A child would not park a brand new bike in his garage only to be used 1 week out of the year! He would ride that bike every chance he could. He would show it to friends and strangers alike, proud of its gleaming paint, handle grips, and reflectors. Likewise, a child receiving the Holy Spirit should not limit the use of his prayer language to 1 week a year at kids camp. He should pray in tongues every day. This is a gift that is meant to be used. Encourage the children who receive the Holy Spirit to pray in tongues each day, live for Jesus, and witness as often as possible.

The question often arises, "Is this really tongues or did I just make this up?" Luke writes, "If you then, though you are evil, know how to give good gifts to your children, how much more will your Father in heaven give the Holy Spirit to those who ask him!" (Luke 11:13). God will not allow a child who sincerely seeks this gift to make it up, or receive a counterfeit. Children can pray and believe with confidence that God will do what He has promised to do.

Children can pray for and counsel other children who wish to receive the Holy Spirit. I often allow boys and girls to pray for their friends. What a faith builder it is for a child to pray and see and hear an immediate response to that prayer. With the laying on of hands children can pray for one another.

If a child does not immediately receive the Holy Spirit, encourage him to continue praying and believing. God will give the Holy Spirit to those who ask. Our heavenly Father knows that perfect special time which a child will receive. A child who has not yet spoken in tongues is not a second class Christian.

When presenting the baptism in the Holy Spirit to children, emphasize the act of drawing near to God. Sometimes children will seek the gift whether they have the giver or not. A boy once asked me to pray that he be filled with the Spirit. After praying a while I asked him if He was a Christian. The boy had never put his faith and trust in Jesus. After praying a sinners prayer he was instantly filled with the Holy Spirit.

I trust that this will help you in leading children into a deeper walk with Jesus. What is the baptism in the Holy Spirit? It is a second gift received after salvation. It is an infilling of power to witness. Children can be filled with the Spirit in your classroom setting. Pray that God will give you wisdom as you venture into this important area of response with the students you serve.

Can Children Minister?

> "It was he who gave some to be apostles, some to be prophets, some to be evangelists, and some to be pastors and teachers, to prepare God's people for works of service, so that the body of Christ may be built up." (Ephesians 4:11,12).

Once children have accepted Christ, they should become involved in ministry training. As a teacher, you have a chance to prepare God's people for works of service. Children can minister. On many occasions, children have prayed with me in class and I have felt the touch of God. I have listened to our kids choir minister and have been touched by God in a new way. Walking through a local shopping mall, I have heard children's voices raised in song and have been refreshed.

Your job description as a teacher does not end with the instilling of godly principles and biblical facts in the little ones you serve. This is only the foundation for the approach that Jesus modeled for every Sunday school teacher. The students are to be trained in ministry. Allow them to serve the Lord with gladness. Help them to prepare lessons for their peers. Let them dramatize a Bible story, give an object lesson, or collect the offering.

Children are part of today's church and should be allowed to minister now. Good habits of ministry become a help to future teachers and to the children themselves. Children can be effective ministers in the classroom, in the church, and in the community.

MINISTRY IN THE CLASSROOM

Children are effective teachers. Children in your class have a developing gift of ministry. Let them use this gift. A child who is allowed to minister in his elementary years will grow into a ministering adult. These children will some day stand by your side as Sunday school teachers, pastors, and missionaries.

When a child reaches the fourth-grade, he usually feels he has heard every song, major Bible story, and illustration. Some children begin around this age to be burned out with the Sunday school experience. They become apathetic at best and at the worst disruptive. A cure for this commonality is involvement. A key to involvement is the investment of your time in prospective ministers. How can a child minister in class?

1. Scripture

We all retain a greater understanding of a theme when we are required to teach that theme. This holds true with children. One of the best ways to instill a memory verse in a child is to employ his assistance in teaching that verse. Let him place the words on the flannel graph, pop the balloons, or lead his peers in repetition of the verse. A child can teach the memory verse in your class.

2. Bible Stories

Children can tell, dramatize, or sing your Bible stories. You may pride yourself in the storytelling technique. Go ahead and tell the story. After you have told it allow the children to take turns retelling it. You will be amazed at how much life a child can put into telling a Bible story.

You may find yourself working on the Bible story with children during the week. Practice lines and movements with them. In some cases spontaneity is better. I have slipped costumes on kids right in class, given them the title of the story and told them to act it out. With no rehearsal, some of the facts may become jumbled. When that occurs they are fed the proper lines and actions and asked to do the story once more. In this way, every child becomes part of the Bible story. You may find one or two children that can tell a story with greater skill than your own. Do not worry, he may be your pastor someday!

3. Music

Children should be allowed to help choose the music used in your classroom. Boys and girls can assist in leading songs, performing special numbers, or operating recording equipment. Music is a big part of many children's lives. Let them minister in music in your classroom. Your encouragement may mark the difference between that child's serving God or serving the other team with his talent.

4. Prayer

Children can be incredible prayer warriors. Let them pray for the sick, for the church, and for their teacher. Children can and should be encouraged to lead in prayer.

These are just some of the ways children can minister. Explore every possibility as you plan future lessons. Let your classroom be a place where children can grow in ministry. Apply yourself to training boys and girls to be ministers.

MINISTRY IN THE CHURCH

Boys and girls can be a blessing to your entire congregation. They can minister in a variety of ways to their peers and those younger and older. Yes, children can even minister to adults. Children can minister in the church in several ways.

1. Leading In Worship

Invite some children to join your worship team. Many churches have a team of three or four adults that lead in congregational worship. Including children on this team will immediately gain the attention of all children present.

2. Ministering With Puppets

Puppets can present songs or skits. Adults as well as children enjoy puppet presentations. Puppets can bring a humorous angle to a message that may not be received by any other form of delivery. Many churches involve children in puppet ministry.

3. Reading Scripture

The Pastor may invite a child to come to the pulpit and read the Scripture text for the evening's sermon. Many children have good reading skills and would gladly participate in this way.

4. Sharing Special Music

Many children in your class and church take instrumental music lessons either privately or through their schools. The public schools will showcase these children in monthly PTA meetings and at local shopping malls. The church rarely makes a place for these kids. Schedule children who have played an instrument a year or longer. When they play in your evening service younger children will be encouraged to begin study and to use this talent for the Lord.

5. Leading In Prayer

A child can be invited to lead in prayer at the beginning, during prayer for the sick, for the offering, or at the conclusion of the service. Children should be encouraged from the pulpit to participate in altar services.

6. Presenting Drama

Occasionally, dramatic skits can emphasize a spiritual truth. Let children to take part in a drama troupe at your church. The whole family will enjoy skits presented by the children.

7. Ushering and Greeting

Children can, under the direction of the regular ushers, serve in this capacity. Don't overdo these kinds of ministries as you want this to remain a special opportunity that children enjoy.

8. Operating Special Equipment

The most common practice I see in this area is a child working the overhead projector. The child can turn it on and change transparencies as required. In one church I noticed children in the sound booth. The church sound man was training children so that they could run sound for their morning children's church service.

9. Sharing Scripture and Testimonies

A pastor I know opens his service each week with prayer. After prayer, he invites any, young or old, to share a meaningful Scripture verse. Many children come ready to quote or read a passage to the entire congregation. This seems to be a fulfillment of 1 Corinthians 14:26 where it says, "What then shall we say, brothers? When you come together, everyone has a hymn, or a word of instruction, a revelation, a tongue or an interpretation. All of these must be done for the strengthening of the church."

Children love to be entrusted with ministry. Look for opportunities to plug them into Christian service in your church. The ministry that begins in your classroom can grow throughout the whole church and spill over into your community.

MINISTRY IN THE COMMUNITY

Ministry in the community begins with ministry in the home. Children should always be encouraged to obey their parents, assist with household chores, and set an example in action, attitude, and speech. The testimony of a child really living for God in his home can affect the entire neighborhood. Children who take on the "mind" of Christ, often times lead their own parents into a closer walk with Jesus.

You cannot, as a Sunday school teacher, control what happens or how a child lives in his home. You can be a consistent source of encouragement for Godly living. Remind children that they are part of God's family. Let them know that you believe in their ability to live for Christ each hour of each day.

Ministry that begins in the home and with the family can spill over into the neighborhood and community. Children who know Christ can be a blessing to their community.

Here are just a few ideas for involving your Sunday school students in ministry in the community.

1. Clean up

Almost every community has some unsightly yard, street corner, or alley that needs a good cleaning. Volunteer to provide the labor needed to accomplish the job. One Sunday school class not only cleaned up a vacant corner lot, but built a park bench, planted flowers, and mowed the lawn each week.

2. Helping hands

Many seniors and others, for one reason or another, are homebound. The children you serve can serve these people. Raking leaves, caring for the lawn, or even painting are all tasks that can be handled by your class. These tasks are accomplished in the spirit of Christian love with no expectation of payment.

Junior-aged children can babysit or even take care of pets for those in their neighborhoods. Perhaps your class can organize childcare for mothers of preschoolers who have little opportunity to get out of the house. Helping hands for those in need is practical living out of Christ's command to "love one another as I have loved you."

3. Special entertainment

Libraries, shopping malls, and city parks can become open doors of ministry for your class. These kinds of locations do not usually allow full-fledged fire and brimstone style preaching. With songs, storytelling, dramatics, clowns, or puppets, your class can provide community service that will turn people towards your church and eventually to Christ. One church on Maui is actually paid to bring their children to sing in shopping malls during the Christmas season.

4. Nursing home

Children need the influence and touch of the elderly. Seniors need the influence and touch of children. What better place to bring the two together than to your local nursing home(s). So many people are placed in the nursing home setting and forgotten. I have watched the activity room come to life as my children have entered and began speaking to the residents. Children can provide an organized program or simply visit.

5. Cable television

Many communities have public access cable networks. What this means for the church is the possibility of utilizing free television time for ministry to your community. Children can be part of such ministry.

A variety of other opportunities exist for children to minister in your community. In my town, the kids participate in local parades, city-wide celebrations and the county and state fairs. In any ministry to the community, you will want to monitor the activity of the children and those they contact. The same basic guidelines followed for any class outing should be observed.

Can children minister? Yes! Children want to minister and they have the ability to bring the joy and love of Jesus to others. They can minister in your class, in the church, and in the community. There was a man in Minnesota who refused to attend church. The mom and the daughters faithfully attended Sunday school and prayed for their dad. The church held its annual Sunday school Christmas program. Family and friends in the community were invited. This unchurched father was so impressed with the ministry of the children, that he came back to our church again and again. He came to Christ through the ministry of his elementary-aged daughters and is now in lay ministry in the church.

Give children the opportunity to minister now, and when they are old they won't depart from it. Train them to serve the Lord with gladness on every front and as they grow they will become the leaders of the church of tomorrow.

You Want Me To Become A Storyteller?

11

"Sunlight had just begun to carve portraits in the morning dew that hung heavy on bent blades of green. A bird darted low over the Green Hills of Kavan in search of a fresh breakfast. Sarabella made her way to the crest of the hill, her feet clothed in dew and dandelion seed. Her pale blue eyes could just make out the Crystal Castle in the distance. "I am going to have my horse shot when I return to the castle," she spat. "Throwing me off and making me walk like, like, a commoner." This was one angry princess, but then she rarely ever smiled. That's why people called her "Sarabella the Rude"[11] behind her back.

Y-ou have just read the beginning of a story. Every book, magazine, newspaper, coffee break, and telephone line is filled with stories. You are a storyteller! That's right. You are a storyteller. Storytelling is a human condition. From the earliest recorded history, people have told stories. The earliest recorded history is a story. In the Sunday school class, children's church, or club ministry you will be called upon to tell both Bible and life application stories. You might even tell a joke or two. You guessed it, jokes are stories!

Jesus was a magnificent teacher. He used a variety of methodology, oftentimes involving the pupil. In all of his mastery as a teacher, Jesus seemed to favor the story. Perhaps this is because a story can touch the heart like no other method. People of Christ's time were challenged, inspired, and changed by His

103

stories. People of our time are still challenged, inspired and changed by his stories.

Think about last week's sermon. Do you remember the points or the stories that made them palatable to you? Chances are, it is because of the illustrations that you remember the points of the sermon. Jesus used parables, history, common situations, and scriptural accounts to state His message with clarity.

In your quest to become the best teacher you can be, you will want to sharpen your natural storytelling skills. I know you will work at this and become a fantastic storyteller. Let's look at basics that must be observed before and during the telling of a story.

Know It

Have you ever heard somebody tell a joke and forget the punch line? The joke just doesn't sound funny. Can you imagine Peter on the day of Pentecost forgetting the story of salvation?

"And a...then a...Jesus...a...was a...How was he killed, John? You were there." Know the story! There is nothing worse for the elementary child than to sit while his teacher struggles through a Bible story. It is embarrassing for the teacher and boring to the student.

I can hardly imagine Jesus with His face locked in the quarterly stuttering through the story of the day. Read and reread the story in your preparation time. Let the story become part of your life. This will come through in your presentation.

Have Confidence

Jesus taught as one having authority. You are God's appointed person for the class you teach. Tell the story with confidence! The authority of the God of the universe rests on you. Confidence in your ability to tell a story comes by prayer, practice, and the power of God. Let yourself tell a story with Godly poise. Godly poise is the sum total of a teacher's posture, attitude, and unwavering confidence as he masterfully weaves the truth of God's love into every story told.

Get Excited!

Enter into the story. Become a participant at the side of Jesus in the boat. Walk through the crowds as the loaves and fishes are handed out. March with the Israelites as Jericho falls. Get excited! Have you ever heard a four-year-old excitedly tell the Bible story of the day? Listen to one in the hallway of your church. The mouth gets to moving so fast the brain can hardly catch up. They will get all of the facts as understood in that story and even add some creative flourish. Can you be that excited? I think so.

Change Your Voice

You don't have to use the same voice for every character in a story. Change your voice. Right now I want you to speak in your normal voice. Say this, "Jesus loves me." Now in the highest voice you can squeak out say, "Jesus loves me." Now in the deepest bass voice say, "Jesus loves me." You have just demonstrated three different voices you can use in this week's story. If there is a narrator make that your normal voice. Use others for the characters. Add an accent and get a whole different sound. In a normal tone say, "Jesus loves you." Add a southern accent and say it again.

Express Feeling

We are Pentecostal people. Others accuse us of showing emotion. So let's show some! You can express feeling. Is the character in the story sad, happy, mad, frustrated? Show these feelings with your face, voice, and posture. Bible stories are full of emotion. A story told with feeling is long remembered.

Practice the Story

Even the best storytellers continue to practice their trade. Practice every story as if it is to be told to Christ Himself. I have found that any story can be improved with practice. As you practice you will learn new ways to express feeling, adjust your tone of voice, and give the story more impact.

FINDING AND TELLING THE STORY

Every week your quarterly includes a Bible story and some type of life application story. Work to become so good at telling these that you do not have to lean heavily on the visualization of them. Children love to hear positive stories from your own childhood. They love any true story that gives practical meaning to the lesson of the day. Choose your stories with the theme of the day in mind. A story told in Sunday school should always point to your theme.

Read It

Read it and reread it! Read the story out loud. Read it into a tape player and listen to yourself reading it. Familiarize yourself with the main points. There is nothing more frustrating for children than the obvious first reading of a story by their teacher in class.

Outline It

Even pastors refer to outlines when preaching. Write a brief outline of the story and practice telling it from this outline. Write the outline on a 3 by 5-inch card, transparency frame or even on the backside of a flannelgraph figure. The outline should be easily read. When telling the story, place your outline where you can refer to it as needed.

Illustrate It

Look for ways to illustrate the story. Involve the children as much as possible when illustrating the story. Keep in mind that children will retain what is learned much longer if it is visualized and if they are actively involved in the learning process. Here are four methods I use in telling stories.

1. Breakfast cereal: Using the overhead projector and ordinary dry cereal, you will tell the story. Choose pieces of cereal to represent each character in the story. These are laid on the overhead and become the body of "shadow puppets" created

when the light is switched on. Move the cereal around as the story dictates, adding characters when required to do so and eating those who leave the story. Children will watch in awe as your cereal shadows give new fun to a well-known story. Finally when the story is finished, eat all of the characters.

2. Splash: This is an overhead projector method. A simple illustration is made with marker on a clear transparency. As the story is told, food coloring is dropped here and there on the transparency. (These drops appear to be dark spots on the projection.) At the climax of the story, a second transparency is placed on the first. The food coloring will spread out making a splash of color on your illustration. Turn off the projector when finished.

3. Action Figures: The story will be dramatized using action figures or little people that a preschooler might play with. Choose a figure to represent each character in the story. Children from the class are invited to come to the front and act out the story by moving the figures around on a table or piano top. You are the narrator giving lines to each character. The children enjoy moving the action figures and speaking their lines. When the story is finished, action figures are collected and children applauded as they return to their seats.

4. Paper Sack Puppets: A group of children will create puppets with various sized paper sacks and crayons. No stage is needed. Puppeteers simply stand before their friends and operate the characters. If uncomfortable with this, have them stand behind a portable chalkboard or projection screen, holding the puppets up above the "stage" for the audience to see. Participants may keep puppets at the conclusion of the story.

Rehearse It

Now that you have chosen and developed your illustrative method, practice telling the story again. You will discover that some visuals are awkward. Others that seemed great don't fit with a particular story. Rehearsal is a good time to make adjustments.

Present It

Once you have followed the previous steps you will be ready to present the story to your class. Present it with confidence. You are God's chosen person for that class. Your faithfulness in preparation will be rewarded as children respond to the theme of the day.

Conclusion

Like Jesus, you are both a teacher and a storyteller. Practice this method. Sharpen this talent so that boys and girls, through your storytelling, will become more like Jesus. The time you give to this method will cause improvement in your total outlook on teaching.

CHAPTER NOTES

[1] William Martin, *First Steps For Teachers* (Springfield, MO.: Gospel Publishing House, 1984), 38.

[2] Billie Davis, *The Dynamic Classroom* (Springfield, MO.: Gospel Publishing House, 1987), 107.

[3] *Radiant Life Curriculum*, A brochure, (Gospel Publishing House, 1445 Boonville Avenue, Springfield, Missouri 65802-1894).

[4] Richard Dresselhaus, *Teaching For Decision* (Springfield, MO.: Gospel Publishing House, 1989), 56.

[5] Ibid, 59.

[6] Ibid, 64.

[7] Stephen Rexroat, *The Sunday School Spirit* (Springfield, MO.: Gospel Publishing House, 1979), 63.

[8] William Martin, *First Steps For Teachers* (Springfield, MO.: Gospel Publishing House, 1984), 63.

[9] National Coalition Against Television Violence Newsletter 1987

[10] Bob Hahn, Christian Education Handout, (Joliet, Illinois: Bob Hahn 1984), 1.

[11] Dick Gruber, *Sleeping Sarabella And The Bible Thumper*, (Farmington, MN: Dick Gruber, ©1980), 1.

APPENDIX

Primary Characteristics

SPIRITUAL CHARACTERISTICS — PRIMARY

COMMON CHARACTERISTICS	WHAT THIS SAYS TO THE TEACHER

Six-Year-Olds

Believe God loves them and helps care for them	Encourage them to believe in God.
Jesus is their friend and helper	Let children tell about Jesus and how He has helped them.
Have a knowledge of right and wrong but not necessarily for them	Talk to them about how right and wrong applies to everyone. Use Scripture verses whenever possible.
Have great faith	Encourage their faith by letting them pray and testify about answered prayer.

Seven-Year-Olds

There is a vagueness as to what is right and wrong	Explain right and wrong from a biblical standard. Allow them to read these Scripture passages for themselves.
Jesus is their friend	Be a Christlike friend to them as well.
Enjoy familiar Bible stories	Do not be afraid to repeat a story. Let children role-play stories.
Like to play Bible games	Use Bible games to reinforce materials being studied.
Like to read easy Bible verses and passages.	Let them read simple Scripture passages relating to the lesson.

SOCIAL CHARACTERISTICS — PRIMARY

COMMON CHARACTERISTICS	WHAT THIS SAYS TO THE TEACHER
Want approval and praise	Give praise and attention for the good.
Want to belong to the "group"	Let them know they are part of your class. Involve children in group settings.
Talk to impress adults	Listen to what they say. Use conversation by relating it to the lesson.
Sensitive to what others think about them	Avoid criticizing in front of classmates. Talk to student privately and in love.

Six-Year-Olds

Like to be first	Explain reasons for taking turns as well as the responsibility of being the leader.
Is just learning to work with others	Use small-group activities in which they can learn to work with others.
Like to be boss	Discourage bossy attitudes. Lead into constructive activities. Be firm, and mean what you say.
Often wants to do many things at once	Allow them to make one choice at a time, then stick with it until finished.
Like to talk	Listen! You may be one of the few adults who listens to the child.

Seven-Year-Olds

Critical of themselves	Avoid criticism. Stress positive things.
Exaggerate	Sort out fact from fantasy. Use what is said to help teach biblical truth.
Are self-centered	Help them to reach beyond themselves and to work with others.
Want to make friends	Encourage them to met classmates. Use class socials to build friendships.
Play a variety of roles	Provide opportunities for self-expression.

PHYSICAL CHARACTERISTICS — PRIMARY

COMMON CHARACTERISTICS	WHAT THIS SAYS TO THE TEACHER
Full of energy	Take advantage of this by using methods such as drama, role-play, Bible games, activity choruses, etc.
Restless	Provide a variety of short activities, interspersed with quiet times. Activity length should be about 10–15 minutes.
Tire easily	Avoid long detailed stories and activities. Take time out to rest.

Six-Year-Olds

Enjoy using their hands	Provide activities where they can use their hands. Art activities and fingerplays are good choices.
Cannot do small detailed work	Do not expect them to complete small detailed or complicated work. Keep all handwork simple.
Enjoy active play and games	Provide fun games that increase learning. Incorporate clear, simple rules.
Lack of well-developed eye-hand coordination	Do not expect perfection.

Seven-Year-Olds

Better coordination of small muscle	Children can do smaller work but still lack the skills to do complicated details.
Need adventure	Use stories that trigger imagination. Special guests, socials, or trips can add adventure to the routine.
Need to achieve and do	Choose activities that can be done without direct adult assistance.
Like to use their hands	Provide positive, constructive activities in which they can use their hands.

MENTAL CHARACTERISTICS — PRIMARY

COMMON CHARACTERISTICS	WHAT THIS SAYS TO THE TEACHER
Concrete thinkers	Avoid the abstract and symbolic.
Live in the present	Children are concerned about what is happening now and not the future.
Have a short attention span	You need to change activities frequently to hold their attention.
Curious	Do not put anything in the classroom they can't touch or handle.
Limited concept of time, space, and distance	Difficulty relating past and future. May confuse characters and events.

Six-Year-Olds

Learn through activities	Provide a variety of things for them to do Everything should relate to the lesson.
Have a hard time choosing what to do.	Give them a limited variety of options. Once they have chosen something, make sure they stick with it.
Needs honest encouragement	Provide them with encouragement based on truth. Do not exaggerate.
Likes to do things for himself	Give 6-year-olds a chance to do things for themselves.
Do not understand the importance of rules	Teach them from the Bible that some rules are meant for everyone.

Seven-Year-Olds

Evaluate conduct by what others are doing	Set standards appropriate for everyone.
Are very creative	Provide activities that encourage creativity and allow it to be exercised.
Enjoy reading	Provide class and individual opportunities for them to read.
Perfectionists	When they "fail," explain it is important to do our best even if it is not perfect.
Want to be accepted by peers	Encourage them to be part of your class. Reinforce positive peer experiences.

EMOTIONAL CHARACTERISTICS — PRIMARY

COMMON CHARACTERISTICS	WHAT THIS SAYS TO THE TEACHER
Needs assurance that he is loved	They need to know you love them. An occasional hug or handshake is in order. Listen to them. Let them know you care.
Sensitive to criticism	Avoid hollering or severe criticism in any form. Look for opportunities to give them praise.

Six-Year-Olds

Lack self-control	Unwritten but understood class rules will help the 6-year-old control himself.
Easily discouraged	Avoid long or difficult activities. Remember they cannot read well.
Feelings change quickly	Taking time out or waiting a few minutes can make all the difference when ministering to a 6-year-old.
Go to pieces in the face of frustration or disappointment	Avoid disappointing circumstances. Encourage rather than criticize.

Seven-Year-Olds

Retreat or a desire to run away is the favored method of dealing with difficulties	Help them learn they cannot run away from problems. Show them that God is present to help in time of trouble or difficulty. Give them encouragement.
May have imaginary or real fears	Let them know God takes care of them.
Try to avoid new or different situations	Do not continually introduce new methodology. Provide a variety of the old interspersed with the new.
Try to be independent but are afraid of making mistakes	Praise them when they succeed. Guide them when you know they are wrong. Do not criticize.
Often boast or exaggerate	Accept what they say but kindly let them know they are exaggerating.

Middler Characteristics

SPIRITUAL CHARACTERISTICS — MIDDLER

COMMON CHARACTERISTICS	WHAT THIS SAYS TO THE TEACHER
One of the easiest groups to lead to Christ	Provide times for the children to respond to the message of Jesus Christ.
Have good memories	Teach the Bible. Help them develop good Bible reading habits. Use the Bible Fact Pak. Keep your promises to them.
Trust God	Find ways to strengthen trust. Involve students in activities that will help them learn about God.

Eight-Year-Olds

Interested in Bible stories and characters	Let them do research into biblical subjects. Use drama and role-play. Show them ways to study the Bible. Use Bible games to reinforce the lesson.
Need help understanding some biblical terms	Explain terms such as grace, sin, and salvation using simple terminology. Keep a Bible dictionary in the classroom.
Need guidance in finding Christ as Savior	Explain salvation. Provide opportunities for children to accept Christ.
Practical in their approach to the Bible. Ask questions.	Speak plainly and simply. When they ask questions answer truthfully. If you do not know, say so.

Nine-Year-Olds

Enjoy attending Sunday school	Make every child feel welcome. Keep the class interesting to encourage a positive attitude towards the church.
Relate Bible stories to their own life experiences	Give personal application with lessons. Ask them to give examples also.
Can work together on projects	Involve them in specific assignments and class projects. Praise good work.
Can participate in deeper worship experiences	Teach proper worship practices and allow time for questions. Provide worship experiences in the classroom.

SOCIAL CHARACTERISTICS — MIDDLER

COMMON CHARACTERISTICS	WHAT THIS SAYS TO THE TEACHER
Friends are important	Find ways of involving everyone in class with each other. Try to develop good self-esteem in each pupil.
Strong sense of fairness and justice	Treat each child equally. Show what the Bible says about how we should treat others. Show that God is fair and just.
Sensitive to criticism	Avoid criticism of individuals. When correction is needed always talk to the individual alone.

Eight-Year-Olds

Will attempt to place blame on others	Show them the wrongness of placing blame on others for something they choose to do.
Can accept responsibilities	Give them a chance to do things for you. Your trust will do much for the children and your effectiveness with them.
Group approval is important	Encourage the children to accept each other and visitors in your class. Provide opportunities for children to get to know each other.
Developing interest in people	A study of real-life missionary characters and biblical heroes will help to satisfy this need. Use Boys and Girls Missionary Crusade materials.
Like to feel grown-up	Make them feel wanted by letting them do and plan things for themselves.

Nine-Year-Olds

Judge fairness and discipline by both their own and the group's standard	Be aware of what the group thinks but do not compromise biblical standards.
Like to be trusted	Trust them to do things they say.
More competitive as group members than as individuals	When planning competitive activities involve the whole group.
Not dependent on praise. Will do something because they want to do it	Thank and praise them. Some need more incentives than a pat on the back.

PHYSICAL CHARACTERISTICS — MIDDLER

COMMON CHARACTERISTICS	WHAT THIS SAYS TO THE TEACHER
Full of energy	Take advantage of this energy by using such methods as role play, drama, Bible games, or active choruses.
Need opportunity to move	Use a variety of short-length activities. Include quiet as well as active projects. Vary your presentations (quiet, active, quiet, etc.). Give opportunity for movement. Maximum activity length should be no longer than 15 minutes.

Eight-Year-Olds

Good eye-hand coordination.	With the ability to do more detailed work, you can plan smaller handwork projects.
Healthier than 6-or 7-year olds	Expect good attendance records.
Enjoys organized games	Use team games to increase learning and express previous achievement. Have clear simple rules.
Prefers tag to toys	Would rather be up and running than sitting with handwork or toys. Plan movement into every lesson.

Nine-Year-Olds

Like to make lists	Try some biblical lists, perhaps as homework. Check interest level before assigning such projects.
Release tension through movement, biting nails, or running fingers through hair	Allow them to stretch. Movement is a 9-year-old's way of coping with growing pains. His muscles need to stretch.
Dependable and responsible	Trust them. Give them responsibility in your classroom.
Like to show their skillfulness	Invite others to see their work. Use their abilities during class time

MENTAL CHARACTERISTICS — MIDDLER

COMMON CHARACTERISTICS	WHAT THIS SAYS TO THE TEACHER
Curious	Bring things to class they can touch and examine. A nature center or special table set aside for investigating objects can be useful in the Middler classroom. Be sure to answer their questions.
Limited concepts of time and distance	Explain new concepts or terms. Use pictures when possible. Be patient. Use language they can understand.
Limited vocabularies	Explain new words. Question to see if they understand what you said.

Eight-Year-Olds

More mature mentally	Lead them in memorizing Scripture verses and doing Bible research.
Eager to learn	Let them participate in class projects.
Creativity is at its peak	Give opportunity for creative expression.
Read well	They can read in class. Encourage them to carry on daily private devotions.
Learning games interest them	Provide games as a means of reviewing the lesson. Games can also be used to help with the memory verse.
Interested in facts and true stories	Do not exaggerate stories. Allow children to research biblical facts

Nine-Year-Olds

Seeking for self-identity and look to adults for role models	They look to see if what they are being taught is being lived by the teacher.
Ready to tackle anything	Give them opportunities to succeed.
Likes details and unusual information	Encourage them to read the Bible and learn its facts. Junior Bible Quiz will help meet this need. Listen to what they say and use it to your advantage.
Watch a lot of television and listen to the radio	They are aware of world events, but cannot always process information received through the media. Fears arise from this.

EMOTIONAL CHARACTERISTICS — MIDDLER

COMMON CHARACTERISTICS	WHAT THIS SAYS TO THE TEACHER
Need adult assurance and recognition	The teacher needs to become sensitive to the needs of each child. Offer praise for things well-done.
Complainers	Listen to each child and hear what he says. Provide encouragement. Act upon those feelings and ideas that a child shares.

Eight-Year-Olds

Resent being bossed	Ask rather than order them to do something. Let them make choices.
Critical of themselves	Give honest encouragement.
Want to do things for themselves	Allow them to do for themselves. It will be hard at times for you, but they need to discover their own capabilities.

Nine-Year-Olds

Are big worriers	Listen to what they are worried about. Try to help them. Let them know Jesus can help them with their problems, both real and imagined.
Relatively easy to discipline	They know when they have done wrong. Accept their apology and don't overreact.
May hate something but will do it anyway	Encourage them to try new things. Praise them for good work.
Curious	Provide them a variety of things to do, touch, and make.
Change in mood and attitude quickly	Wait a while before you react. Accept them as they are.

Junior Characteristics

SPIRITUAL CHARACTERISTICS — JUNIOR

COMMON CHARACTERISTICS	WHAT THIS SAYS TO THE TEACHER
Need to feel the church they are attending is their church too	Introduce them to church leadership. Teach them about membership.
Have a good memory and eager to learn	Provide them with sound and challenging Scripture verses.
Many accept Christ at this age	Provide opportunities for accepting Christ. Give doctrinal training also.
Many receive the baptism in the Holy Spirit	Provide instruction and opportunity to receive this gift.

Ten-Year-Olds

They seek heroes	Provide them with stories, books, or videos of Christian heroes.
Aware of their need to please God through prayer and Bible reading	Let them pray. Encourage daily devotions. Explain stories simply and honestly try to answer questions.
Can help others	A class project helping someone encourages this.
Realize the importance of God in their future plans	Answer questions about the future. Encourage students to pray and read the Bible when searching for answers.
Are influenced by teachers	Be a good example. Live a life consistent with what you teach.

Eleven-Year-Olds

Realize value of relationships	Take interest in them. Encourage proper selection of friends. Jesus is their friend
Seek guidance from God	Show them how.
Learning to use study helps	Provide concordances and other study helps. Guide them in how to use these.
Look to the Bible for answers	Direct them toward resources that tell them how to find biblical answers.
Ask searching questions	Answer questions honestly. Research questions you cannot answer.
Are influenced by teachers	Be a good example

SOCIAL CHARACTERISTICS — JUNIOR

COMMON CHARACTERISTICS	WHAT THIS SAYS TO THE TEACHER
Resent adults talking down to them	Juniors want to be treated as adults, not as children. Treat them as equals. Give them the same respect you wish to receive from them.
Have a strong sense of justice.	Juniors will watch how you, the teacher, act. Be a good example. Teach them that God is faithful and just. Show them what the Bible says about these things.
Are influenced by their peer group	Group acceptance is important and should be recognized. Allow times for them to work with others who may not be part of their group.

Ten-Year-Olds

Concerned about relationships with parents and peer group	Explain that both groups are important.
Enjoy team games as well as group activities	Provide for team competition. Junior Bible Quiz can help fill this need.
Ready to discuss simple social problems	They are aware of their world. Discuss ways your Sunday school class can help in the community.

Eleven-Year-Olds

Are keen competitors and will often compete with others to gain recognition	Show them the right and wrong ways to compete. Discuss what the Bible says about competition.
Are interested in social problems.	Discuss problems in the community as they arise. Find ways they can be involved both in and out of Sunday school.

PHYSICAL CHARACTERISTICS — JUNIOR

Common Characteristics	What This Says To The Teacher
Are doers and tend to overdo themselves	Provide things for Juniors to do. Give them choices and help them to finish one thing before moving on to another.
Are in the healthiest time of their lives	Expect them to attend Sunday school on a regular basis.
Have longer attention span	Activities can be longer. More time is spent on the lesson. Carry activities over from week to week if necessary.

Ten-Year-Olds

Are cooperative with adults	Work with them. Bring adults into your class to share with the Juniors.
May be restless and tired at times	A physical change is beginning.
Girls are more developed physically	Girls are typically more mature than boys by about a year. Some girls will be self-conscious. Be sensitive to individual needs.

Eleven-Year-Olds

Boys are more restless.	Allow some moving around.
Able to care for themselves	Be a guide rather than a leader. Let them discover and do things for themselves.
May complain of being tired	They are changing physically. Provide physical activity and rest periods.

MENTAL CHARACTERISTICS — JUNIOR

COMMON CHARACTERISTICS	WHAT THIS SAYS TO THE TEACHER
Are good readers. They spend leisure time reading.	Provide Christian books to be borrowed and returned.
Like challenge	Stimulate interest through such things as puzzles, contests, quizzes, and codes.
Have a great imagination and like to think	Channel their intellectual energy into something creative.
Developed sense of time and distance	Discuss more Bible facts and places. This is a good age to introduce the use of maps when explaining biblical places.
Like to take part in group planning	Allow group to participate in planning socials and class events.
Are more self-motivated	Give instructions and let them do work in the classroom on their own.

Ten-Year-Olds

Are creative persons.	Direct their creativity into drama, songs, art, and other participatory methods. Be sure these relate to the lesson.
Respond to visual stimuli	Use posters, charts, and pictures.
Can work without adult supervision	Let them do things by themselves. Allow more freedom in classroom. However, never leave the classroom unattended.
Open to new ideas. Golden year for ideas and ideals.	Present high ideals but things you can live up to as well. You are their example.
Are developing talents	Take advantage of their abilities and curiosity in your teaching.

Eleven-Year-Olds

Enjoy creating stories, poems, drama and art.	Use a variety of methodology. Let them plan and accomplish tasks.
Approaching age of idealism.	Show them Jesus is the person to follow.
Want adult acceptance	Give unconditional acceptance. Do not talk down to them.
Are curious, enthusiastic, and honest	Provide activities that inspire curiosity and enthusiasm. Compliment honesty.
Will daydream about later events	Do not scold for daydreaming. Help them to understand future events as outlined in the Scripture.

EMOTIONAL CHARACTERISTICS — JUNIOR

COMMON CHARACTERISTICS | WHAT THIS SAYS TO THE TEACHER

Common Characteristics	What This Says To The Teacher
Like to complain	Don't scold. Accept what they have to say. It's probably right anyway.
Able to make choices	Give them things to do. Offer choices of activities whenever possible.
Can get absorbed in doing something and won't hear you talking	This comes naturally. Channel their energy into creative things, then let them become absorbed in these. Do not insist on a strict schedule. Be flexible.

Ten-Year-Olds

Happy with themselves	They are happy with themselves and the teacher should be too. You probably won't have as great a discipline problem as with 9-year-olds.
Are cooperative, outgoing, friendly, agreeable	Take advantage of this change. Give them things to do.
Are critical of themselves	The child will be happy one minute and overly critical the next. Assure them they are okay and are doing fine. If they are not doing well, encourage them.

Eleven-Year-Olds

Experience unsteady emotions and may be moody	Accept them. They are undergoing emotional changes and at times cannot help themselves. Your understanding will help.
Idealistic with high standards set for themselves and others	They will expect you to live up to standards they have set. Teach them Christ's standards for living.